A Behavioural
Approach to the
Management of Stress

WILEY SERIES ON
STUDIES IN OCCUPATIONAL STRESS

Series Editors

Professor Cary L. Cooper
Department of Management Sciences,
University of Manchester Institute
of Science and Technology

Professor S. V. Kasl
Department of Epidemiology,
School of Medicine,
Yale University

Stress at Work
Edited by Cary L. Cooper and Roy Payne

Current Concerns in Occupational Stress
Edited by Cary L. Cooper and Roy Payne

White Collar and Professional Stress
Edited by Cary L. Cooper and Judi Marshall

Stress, Work Design and Productivity
Edited by E. N. Corlett and J. Richardson

A Behavioural Approach to the Management of Stress
by H. R. Beech, L. E. Burns, and B. F. Sheffield

Further titles in preparation

A Behavioural Approach to the Management of Stress

A Practical Guide to Techniques

H. R. Beech
The University Hospital of South Manchester

L. E. Burns
Rochdale Area Health Authority

B. F. Sheffield
Salford Area Health Authority

JOHN WILEY & SONS

Chichester · New York · Brisbane · Toronto · Singapore

British Library Cataloguing in Publication Data:

Main entry under title:

A Behavioural approach to the management of stress.

(Wiley series on studies in occupational stress)
Includes indexes.
1. Stress (Psychology)   2. Behavior modification.
I. Beech, H. R.   II. Burns, Laurence, E.   III. Sheffield,
B. F.   IV. Series.

BF575.S75B37 1982 158'.1   81-11554

ISBN 0 471 10054 4   AACR2

Phototypeset by Dobbie Typesetting Service, Plymouth, Devon, England
Reprinted in Great Britain

Contents

Editorial Foreword to the Series

This book, *A Behavioural Approach to the Management of Stress*, is the fifth book in the series of *Studies in Occupational Stress*. The main objective of this series of books is to bring together the leading international psychologists and occupational health researchers to report on their work on various aspects of occupational stress and health. The series will include a number of books on original research and theory in each of the areas described in the initial volume, such as Blue Collar Stressors, The Interface Between the Work Environment and the Family, Individual Differences in Stress Reactions, The Person-Environment Fit Model, Behavioural Modification and Stress Reduction, Stress and the Socio-technical Environment, The Stressful Effects of Retirement and Unemployment and many other topics of interest in understanding stress in the workplace.

We hope these books will appeal to a broad spectrum of readers — to academic researchers and postgraduate students in applied and occupational psychology and sociology, occupational medicine, management, personnel, etc. — and to practitioners working in industry, the occupational medical field, mental health specialists, social workers, personnel officers, and others interested in the health of the individual worker.

CARY L. COOPER,
University of Manchester Institute of
Science and Technology (UK)
STANISLAV V. KASL,
Yale University

Editorial Foreword to the Series

Chapter 1

Occupational Stress and Stress Reactions

For centuries stressful events have been recognized as important components in the development of a variety of adverse conditions and of illnesses. Today's high-pressure lifestyles can take a heavy toll in decreased productivity, frustration, disease and even early mortality. The reactions of individuals to stressors represent a major psychological and medical problem; any attempt to assess the cost presents a formidable task. One estimate, made in the United States, indicates that the direct costs of executive stress alone are nearly $20 billion per year. Direct costs refer to lost days at work, in- and out-patient treatment and executive deaths. Indirect costs are even more difficult to estimate and include items such as impaired motivation, poor decision-making, loss of creativity and accidents.

When direct and indirect costs of blue-collar stress are considered, manifestations of which may be discontent, absenteeism, high turnover and poor quality of work, the problem begins to take on major proportions. Add to these considerations problems caused by alcoholism and drug abuse and it becomes apparent that the estimate of $20 billion is no more than the tip of the financial iceberg. Given then the magnitude of the problem, what are the main sources of stressors within the work place?

TYPES OF OCCUPATIONAL STRESSORS

Work fulfils a number of basic human needs. Stress may arise when there is a failure to satisfy these needs or when there is a perceived threat to their satisfaction.

Work, of course, provides income which enables us to purchase material goods essential for our survival and comfort. It provides purposeful physical and mental activity. Self-esteem and feelings of competence may be increased. Finally, it can meet some social needs by providing opportunities for social contact.

1

Types of occupational stressors include the following:

(A) Problems of work load

(1) *Work overload*

Overload has deservedly received much attention as an important stressor. The job demands are such as to exceed the individual's perceived ability to meet the demands. Several types of overload may be identified.

(i) *Quantitative overload*   This type exists when the individual has too much work to do in a given period of time. He may be fully competent in his work but the time restriction is what elicits the stress reaction. Quantitative overload could involve working for long hours without appropriate rest periods, as with excessive overtime. It can be created by an inability to complete work due to frequent interruptions or by the imposition of unrealistic deadlines.

Most organizations have some form of time pressure over their employees—deadlines for unit production quotas on an assembly line, deadlines for work projects, deadlines for reports, et cetera. Chronic time urgency can lead to overarousal with the consequence that the cardiovascular system may be adversely affected (Friedman and Rosenman, 1974).

(ii) *Qualitative overload*   Stressful reactions due to this type of stressor may result when the work exceeds the technical or intellectual competence of the individual. The work may demand continuous concentration, innovation and meaningful decisions. An important factor contributing to qualitative overload is job complexity. The higher the inherent difficulty of the work, which may require a great deal of sophisticated information and high-level academic skills, the more stressful the job. This form of overload may be experienced by individuals working in research and development organizations. Professionals in health care, law, et cetera, are also subject to this type of overload. A consequence of this stressor, wherever it is present, is emotional and mental fatigue, gastrointestinal disorders and headaches.

(iii) *Combination of quantitative and qualitative overload*   In some job situations there is a combination of both quantitative and qualitative overload; this is frequently encountered, for example, in air traffic controllers at busy airports; in this work stressfulness may be directly related to the multi-faceted nature of decision-making which may be a function of the importance of the consequences of the decision, its complexity, the adequacy of the information available, the amount of time available for the decision-making process, and the like. Quantitative and qualitative overload may frequently occur in management and administrative positions.

(2) *Work underload*

Underload may also present difficulties as a job may fail to provide meaningful stimulation or adequate reinforcement. Thus, jobs which involve dehumanizing monotony, no opportunity to use acquired skills and expertise, an absence of any intellectual involvement and repetitive performance provide instances of underload. Boredom can result from too high a degree of specialization. Hans Selye, the father of research into stress, refers to these problems as deprivational stress. The regimentation and discipline of assembly-line work is an example. Reactions to these types of stressors include hysteria where there are incidents of mass industrial outbreaks of illness consisting of nausea, headaches, general malaise and visual dysfunction. Other reactions may include poor productivity, absenteeism and high turnover. Even cases of assembly-line sabotage have been reported. Research indicates that the problem of underload may be accentuated where there are few opportunities for workers to communicate. One consequence of deprivational stress is that employees work at minimally acceptable levels showing no real interest in the work during the week, while at the weekend they engage in avocational pursuits as a compensation device. Such an attitude can have an adverse effect on the organization and can be traced back to poor job satisfaction.

(B) Problems of occupational frustration

Stress reactions may result when the job actually blocks or inhibits the attainment of goals. There are a number of important components of occupational frustration:

(1) *Role ambiguity*

This condition exists when the individual has insufficient information to perform his job satisfactorily. Thus, he may be unclear about the work procedures or objectives; he may be uncertain about the scope and responsibilities of his job. Confusion may exist as to what others expect from him. He may not know precisely how he fits into the organization and lines of accountability may be unclear. There may be a lack of feedback on his performance and he may be unsure of any reinforcement no matter how well he performs. Predictably, such conditions can result in job dissatisfaction and significant stress reactions.

(2) *Role conflict*

This condition exists when the job of the individual contains roles or responsibilities which may directly conflict with each other. Thus, there may be conflicting job demands, differences of view of superiors or problems related to conflicts with personal, professional or societal values.

It appears that role conflict is most commonly seen in middle managers who find themselves trapped between top-level management and lower-level management. Clearly, role conflict can result in stress reaction due to frustration and job dissatisfaction.

(3) *High degrees of specialization*

Some jobs in industry call for a high degree of specialization the goal of which is innovation, increased efficiency and improved quality of work. However, overspecialization can lead to occupational frustration. The individual may feel that he is too far removed from the end product. There is too little opportunity to identify with the company, its policies and products.

(4) *Poor career development guidance*

A major source of stress reactions from occupational frustration may exist when there is a lack of career guidance. The individual needs not only an opportunity to use pre-existing occupational skills but also an opportunity to develop new appropriate skills, the acquisition of which may contribute to increased reinforcement in the work environment. When occupational frustration exists due to a lack of career development guidance there is a need for formal counselling programmes to be developed within the company.

(5) *Poor communication*

There are many networks through which communications flow in an organization. Poor communication is the most frequently reported single major source of frustration in companies. Good decision-making, adequate planning and organization function depend on effective communication. Frustration may result if the only communication channel open is in the downward direction from top management. Clearly there is a need for communication to flow up from lower levels and horizontally from department to department. Effective communication can lead to increased job satisfaction and improved motivation and performance.

(6) *Problems of bureaucracy*

A furtive source of occupational frustration is bureaucracy. As originally conceptualized by Max Weber, bureaucracy aimed to develop sets of rules governing all aspects of organizational behaviour leading to stability and uniformity; organizational relationships should be typified by objectivity and a structure which follows the principle of centralized hierarchy. However, criticisms of this form of organizational structure include the views that it stifles personal and professional development, it promotes and accommodates mediocrity on the job, interferes with effective communication and creativity, and it develops rules which it may be virtually impossible to alter.

(C) Occupational change

Ubiquitous stressors encountered in the work place are change and adaptation; these stressors are inherent in any organization concerned with growth and productivity. Clearly, how the individual perceives the change is important; it is much easier to adjust to change that is thought of as being beneficial but any change can be stressful. Change can be distressful because it disrupts behavioural, physiological and cognitive patterns of functioning and because it requires adaptation. The most important forms of occupational change include:

(1) *Scientific developments*

Computers and other technological advances are contributing to increased efficiency in a variety of work functions from top-level management decisions to office processes. Little consideration, so far, has been given to the role changes for those who are affected. Jobs may become obsolete and new training may be required; clearly some level of adaptation will be necessary and may involve stress reactions.

(2) *Promotion*

Another source of adaptive stress reactions is promotion, and will be thought of by most people as a small price to pay for the rewards of past performance and recognition. Inherent in promotion are several factors involving change. Promotion almost certainly will lead to important changes in job function which may involve increased responsibility for people and production. Accountability to higher levels of management is a likely consequences of promotion, as are changes in social roles. Whether these factors are viewed as positive or negative, they require adaptation.

(3) *Relocation*

Adaptive stress reactions may be involved when moving to a new area, either vocational or residential. Changing to a new residential environment, following promotion, may evoke stressful responses because of the severing of interpersonal relationships, the physical problems of moving possessions and of finding a suitable home, the adjustment needed to a new area and, possibly, culture, new interpersonal relationships and different socioeconomic conditions. Although such changes may be stimulating, nevertheless adaptive energy is required and, therefore, such changes are stressful.

(4) *Organizational restructuring*

Company takeovers and mergers frequently mean new management styles and change in key executive and managerial positions which may have far-reaching effects. Such reorganization can be a major source of stress reactions, resulting in feelings of insecurity and apprehension.

(5) *Redundancy*

It is not difficult to comprehend why redundancy can evoke considerable stress reactions. Consequences of redundancy may be financial insecurity, poor self-esteem and depression. Professor Harvey Brenner of Johns Hopkins University, Baltimore, in discussing the relationship between redundancy and ill health, notes that, in the United States, each increase in unemployment of 1 per cent causes about 37,000 deaths over the succeeding 6 years due to cardiovascular problems, stress-promoted suicide, et cetera. However, it is likely that the vast majority of the costs affect society in the illness area, not the deaths.

(6) Retirement

A final source of adaptive stress is related to the adjustment of retirement. Usually an employee has spent the greater part of his life working; there is frequently a relationship between a man's self-esteem and his work. Thus, when he retires, particularly if he retires from a job providing a great deal of reinforcement, the consequences are likely to include a loss of self-esteem and a feeling of worthlessness, a depressed state, decreased appetite and sexual drive, sleep disturbance, an increase in physical complaints generally, apathy and a loss of motivation. Unfortunately, many workers who are forcibly retired live on average only 2–3 years after their retirement. Factors determining the stressfulness of retirement include preparation for the event, alternative sources of reinforcement (hobbies, social contacts, and the like), and financial security.

(D) Other sources of occupational stressors

Apart from the three broad categories discussed above—problems of load, occupational frustration and occupational change—there are many other possible sources of occupational stressors. The physical environment in which the individual works is crucial. Noise can prove stressful in jobs requiring concentration. In addition to the frequency and the intensity of the noise, other important parameters are its variability and whether it is intermittent. Sound levels above 70 decibels result in sympathetic nervous system arousal. Further increases in the sound level result in an elevated heart rate and increased blood pressure. Chronic decibel levels above 85 may result in permanent hearing loss. Almost certainly, work performance will deteriorate when an individual is directly exposed to chronic noise; this may manifest itself in decreased vigilance and concentration and in a decreased ability to integrate information and perform analytical functions. There may also be increased error and accident rates.

Too little or too much lighting within the work environment may result in stress reactions. Thus, when the illumination is below a minimum level, eye strain may be a consequence with the result that tension headaches may occur. Glare, of course, is another problem and is often a characteristic of too much light. Working conditions in which the temperature is too high or too low can evoke stress responses. Temperature in excess of 80 degrees Fahrenheit affect tasks involving concentration, complex mental manipulations and fine detail. High humidity will significantly compound the problem. At the other extreme of temperature (below 55 degrees Fahrenheit), as the limbs become cold, there is a loss of fine motor co-ordination and manual tasks are hindered.

A frequent source of stressors in the work setting relates to poor interpersonal relationships. Stress may result from feelings of being unaccepted or a failure to recognize particular expertise which the individual feels he possesses. It may also arise from feelings of being discriminated against by influential individuals or the organization itself. Authoritarian individuals making unreasonable demands may evoke frustration or overt or covert hostility. Of course, some jobs involving relationships with clients may be inherently stressful. For example, individuals working in such places as public relations departments, or Social Security offices, may have to contend with a considerable amount of aggression.

Having looked at possible stressors within the work place consideration will now be given to the effects of stressors on the individual.

THE EFFECTS OF STRESSORS ON THE INDIVIDUAL

It is only since the 1920s, following the systematic investigations of the eminent Harvard physiologist Walter B. Cannon, and other physiologists, that the importance of hormones and chemical mediators in the body's response to stressors has been recognized. As the body prepares to defend itself against a threat or to avoid the threat three systems are most directly involved: the cardiovascular, the digestive and the muscular. Examples of the effects of stressors on these systems are summarized in Table 1. The stress response includes an increase of the blood supply primarily to the heart and muscles; there is an increase in the heart rate; the blood pressure is elevated and adrenalin and a related hormone, noradrenalin, is released into the blood supply from the

Table 1   Examples of the effects of stressors on the cardiovascular, digestive and muscular systems

Cardiovascular	Heart rate elevated. Increased blood pressure. Increased heart rate variability. Coronary heart disease.
Digestive	Burning sensation in stomach, chest and throat areas (due to increased stomach acidity). Nausea. Loss of appetite. Reduction in the flow of saliva. Ulcers. Disruption of rhythmic peristalis (making swallowing difficult, diarrhoea, et cetera).
Muscular	Tense muscles. Tension headaches. Tightness of chest cavity. Spasms of the oesophagus/colon (Diarrhoea/constipation). Backache. Tension at back of neck. Tension around the stomach.

adrenal glands. Concurrently, the absorption of food from the digestive system is reduced while energy-producing substances, such as sugar and fats, are released to meet a need for an increased energy supply. The muscular system becomes activated, ready to meet the challenge. Of course, almost every system of the body is involved, to a greater or lesser extent, in the stress response; for example, the respiratory system may be affected in that the respiration rate increases.

In 1936 Hans Selye introduced his concept of stress as the 'General Adaptation Syndrome'; this term referred to the physiological reactions brought about by a broad range of environmental stimuli. In order to differentiate the aetiological factors from the physiological responses Selye used the term 'stressors' for the causative factors. Accordingly, he regarded stress as the non-specific response of the body to any demand and a stressor as a stimulus which evokes stress at any time.

Selye's General Adaptation Syndrome has three phases. The first phase is the alarm response in which the stress is generalized and is manifested by increased activity in most of the body systems. The second phase is referred to as the resistance phase; adaptation to the stressor appears to be localized in one or two of the bodily systems with little or no evidence of the development of symptoms. In the final stage, the exhaustion phase, the system or systems appear to be overloaded with the consequent development of symptoms; thus there is a clear manifestation of stress and this phase can result in illness or even mortality. Selye notes that the adaptation may lead to a disease of adaptation with resultant secondary deterioration.

Since Selye's definition of stress there have been over 110,000 scientific publications related to stress. Unfortunately, Selye's attempt to differentiate aetiological factors from the physiological responses has not been followed by the majority of researchers and writers, who have used physiological stress for the causative factors without indicating a separate term for the stress response. Thus, at present, the cause and the response are both referred to as stress by different researchers. Apart from problems of operational definition there are many other problems: a multiplicity of theories have been advanced to account for stress; few have strong experimental underpinnings; unvalidated explanations abound. These problems have been further compounded by the use of jargon unique to each of the disciplines involved. For our purposes stress may be considered as a response to a stressor that induces a change in the individual's ongoing behavioural, physiological or cognitive patterns of functioning; note that no judgement is made as to the valence of the stressful reaction. The effects of stressors can be either negative or positive; the former aspects will be of most concern in this and forthcoming chapters.

The differential effects of stressors have long been recognized by researchers in the field. Selye distinguishes between the positive, creative and motivating aspects which he refers to as Eustress and the negative, debilitating and aversive ones which he calls Distress. The amount of stress is of importance. As a general rule, as the level of arousal increases, performance also increases; thus the individual is well motivated and he functions at an optimal level. However, when the arousal becomes excessive, performance deteriorates and the functioning becomes disrupted.

Stressors can affect the individual at a cognitive level. His thinking may become more rigid and more concrete. Irrational, self-defeating and ruminative patterns of thought may be a consequence.

Thus it can be observed that the stress response involves three major levels: the physiological, the behavioural and the cognitive. Table 2

Table 2   The stress response—physiological, behavioural and cognitive
aspects

Physiological	Heart rate increased. Blood pressure elevated. Muscular tension. Slowing down of digestive system. Adrenalin and noradrenalin released.
Behavioural	Decreased performance level. Avoidance of stressful situations. Passivity/inertia.
Cognitive	Distortions of thinking. Lowered intellectual functioning. Unproductive, ruminative, anxiety-generating patterns of thinking. Indecisiveness.

summarizes some of the effects at each level. Whether or not stressors produce problems for the individual depends on a multiplicity of factors. In addition to the intensity of the stressors, their nature, range, frequency of occurrence and duration are important; the context or circumstance in which the stressors appear is clearly of significance; the perception of the degree of threat on the part of the individual is crucial as is his repertoire and utilization of adaptive coping skills. Personality factors may contribute to adverse reactions.

As we have seen, the range of potential occupational (and, indeed, other) stressors is large. Rahe and Arthur (1978) developed a rating scale containing 43 items of recent experiences involving change. The various events were numerically rated according to their potential for causing disease. For example, divorce rates as 73 units, marital separation as 65 units, and so on. According to these and other researchers, various types of life-change events often antedate physical illnesses such as heart attacks, ulcers, and the like. The more intense the life-change events and the higher the frequency of occurrence, the greater the probability for a severe reaction to occur. A total of 200 or more units in 1 year is considered to be predictive of the possibility of an individual becoming seriously ill. However, it should be born in mind that these are statistical correlations; not everyone exposed to potent stressors will necessarily develop a stress-related illness.

Personality factors can exacerbate stressful reactions. The evidence for this comes from the work of the two cardiologists mentioned previously, Friedman and Rosenman (1974), who categorized people into Type A and Type B personalities.

Four main characteristics are considered important in Type A personalities:

(1) Multiple behaviour patterns. This refers to the tendency to undertake two or more tasks concurrently; a consequence of this pattern is a failure to complete the tasks satisfactorily.

(2) Time urgency. The tendency is to habitually programme too much work into a limited period of time; this race against the clock is often inappropriate as there may be little rational reason to act in this way.

(3) Inappropriate aggression, hostility and competitiveness. Frequent displays of aggression are common, often in response to minor provocation or frustration. Excessive competitive activity is frequently observed whether the activity is a sporting contest or a discussion.

(4) Poorly defined goals. The tendency is to rush into work without defining objectives and the means by which these will be attained. The consequence may be unfinished work or work which contains errors.

Thus, Type A patterns involve many features: an eagerness to compete, a desire for recognition, quickness of physical and mental functioning, a fierce drive towards poorly defined objectives, self-imposed deadlines, anguish at repetitive chores, multiple thinking and acting, impatience at rate of progress of events, a sense of unease or guilt at relaxing and rapid overt behaviours (walking, eating, talking, et cetera).

Type B patterns involve passivity or not being overly ambitious, restraint and not being prone to develop stress-related disorders.

Friedman and Rosenman believe that individuals with Type A personalities are predisposed to develop premature coronary heart disease. Their research on 3411 men aged 39–59 years showed that, within the 39–49 age group, 85 per cent of those who developed coronary heart disease were originally diagnosed as having Type A personalities. Thus, the cardiovascular system appears to be particularly affected by this constellation of behaviours; studies indicate that Type A individuals, in response to social stressors, have significantly higher systolic blood pressure, heart rate and heart variability when compared to non-Type A's. Many young executives have their behaviours shaped into the Type A pattern as they feel that these are the ones necessary for success in the business world. Thus, the individual is rewarded by a sense of achievement and recognition; also, possibly, promotion.

It is difficult to determine the precise relationship of stress to the incidence of coronary heart disease because of the many confounding variables but there seems little doubt that stress is a very important contributor.

Although coronary artery disease is, by far, the most important of the stress-related diseases there are other prominent diseases believed to be related to stress; these include ulcers, ulcerative colitis and asthma; a summary of these disorders is listed in Table 3. Again, it needs to be

Table 3   Examples of stress-related diseases and conditions

Cardiovascular system	Coronary artery distress.
	Hypertension.
	Strokes.
	Rhythm disturbances of the heart.
Muscular system	Tension headaches.
	Muscle contraction backache.
Locomotor system	Rheumatoid arthritis.
	Related inflammatory diseases of connective tissue.
Respiratory and allergic disorders	Asthma.
	Hay fever.
Immunological disorders	Lowered resistance.
	Autoimmune diseases.
Gastrointestinal disturbances	Ulcer.
	Irritable bowel syndrome.
	Diarrhoea.
	Nausea and vomiting.
	Ulcerative colitis.
Genitourinary disturbances	Diuresis.
	Impotence.
	Frigidity.
Dermatological diseases	Eczema.
	Neurodermatitis.
	Acne.
Other problems	Fatigue and lethargy.

borne in mind that many of these disorders are multi-determined. Although the role of stress cannot be overemphasised in their aetiology and maintenance, other factors are also of significance; these factors include genetic predispositions, excessive smoking, over-use of drugs, too high an intake of alcohol, lack of exercise and poor nutrition.

In view of the potentially serious consequences of prolonged stress reactions, ideally the stressors should be removed or modified wherever possible. However, in many instances it is not possible to make significant changes; in such cases the individual may ameliorate or eliminate the harmful effects of occupational stressors by using stress management techniques while still retaining efficiency and meeting organizational demands. The remainder of this book will be concerned with methods which may be used to achieve these goals.

Chapter 2

The Behavioural Approach

One of the very real problems facing the purveyor of psychological help is that of overcoming existing attitudes and beliefs about the state of the art, since much of our information about such matters has derived from cinema or TV portrayals of the psychiatrist or psychologist rather than from any authoritative source. One has no objection at all, of course, to Sigmund Freud being presented as quite human in domestic situations (by and large, psychiatrists and psychologists possess their fair share of human feeling) although Montgomery Clift's role as Freud produces the memorable line from his screen wife, 'Is anything the matter, Siggy dear?' Maybe Mrs Freud *did* call her illustrious husband Siggy and maybe she *did* worry about his preoccupation with the convoluted mysteries of sexual thoughts, and maybe we shouldn't be too offput by Hollywood's best endeavours.

On the other hand one is prompted to react more sensitively to the creation of quite illusory notions about the human psyche—for example, that there is an early trauma lurking beneath every neurotic reaction—the notion that we are anxious as adults because of something that happened in the woodshed at an early and formative age. Hollywood certainly cherishes this basic idea and 'psychological' epics set out to show that getting rid of our problems must involve identifying some historically distant cause, tracking down this remote event and bringing it to the contemporary conscious mind of the sufferer.

Hence, such sagas often are indistinguishable in form from the standard detective movie; no doubt entertaining, but having little or nothing to do with the true state of affairs.

Another aspect of the entertainment world's view of psychological treatment would seem to have rather more political overtones or, at least, to reflect the special views of the author or director. 'Clockwork Orange' is a good example of one lay view of behavioural treatment and is as distorted in its own way as is a version of a Viennese psychiatrist played by Benny Hill. At least in part this book is an attempt to redress

15

the balance by presenting a factual account of a contemporary approach to stress treatment and control. In it, we hope, those concerned with or affected by stress problems will identify the kind of logic and factual basis that will make a refreshing alternative to the parody provided by films and TV.

The Behavioural approach attempts to avoid making mysterious that which can be made plain. Not always, one must point out, with a comforting message to offer since the plain unvarnished truth is that we do not have answers to many of the pressing human problems that cry out for attention; yet, at least, it can be said that we know well what we do know and it is this body of information that is worth documenting as it leads to useful practical action.

With some notable exceptions Hollywood and TV versions of psychological treatment are primarily concerned with the portrayal of Psychoanalysis; indeed, Psychoanalysis has become the generally accepted synonym for psychological treatment and, in popular parlance 'being psychoanalysed' has come to mean (half jokingly) being *really* understood. So much is this the case that few of us may even get around to asking just how much evidence there is in favour of Psychoanalysis, let alone whether there are any alternatives. Amazingly, the public generally bring an uncritical gaze to the psychological treatment scene and display a trust and acceptance of the Hollywood myths that they would certainly not bring to the scrutiny of vegetables or motor cars. No doubt this is all quite understandable in that psychological mechanisms are thought to be too complex for the lay mind to grasp (unlike cars or vegetables), or that such matters can be left entirely to the expert who knows what he is doing or selling (unlike the greengrocer or car salesman who may need a little help from the general public).

In our opinion the public at large *should* be viewing psychological treatment with a critical eye and, hopefully, will bring to that appraisal a set of standards not unlike those they may be used to exercising in choosing a car or their weekend shopping. In short, adopting the view that deciding what is good and bad respecting psychological treatment is as much a question of facts about performance as is the selection of one's next motor car. Of course, some people will still be disposed to judge in terms of superficial appearances, tradition or merely blind faith, but others may elect to view the issue in a more objective and rational way. The bases for making such judgements are perhaps best understood in the light of the background to and development of Behaviourism.

Watson (1878–1958), the founder of American Behaviourism, had become entirely disenchanted with the 'intangibles and unapproachables' of Psychology and set out to create a Psychology that dealt with concrete facts. Accordingly, he urged a redefinition of psychology as the 'science of behaviour' that would be a purely objective experimental branch of natural science with the objective of predicting and controlling observable behaviour. In essence he was urging psychology to be less 'armchair', less philosophical, less vague, less anthropomorphic in the interests of becoming much more rigorous, objective and scientific. Indeed, during the 1920s Watson's ideas achieved considerable popularity, perhaps very particularly because of his scorn for the mysterious mental mechanisms postulated by others and his attempts to build a science of psychology from observables rather than intangibles—someone who would bring clarity, rigour and real progress to the area. His claims, for the time certainly, were quite substantial since he felt strongly that the application of Pavlovian conditioning could produce all manner of previously unexpected changes and his report on Little Albert exemplified this contention.

Briefly, Little Albert was a stolid 11-month-old baby exposed by Watson to an experimental situation in which the possibility of acquiring (learning) emotional reactions was to be considered. Basically, the question posed was that of whether a simple conditioning process could produce a learned fear in this child.

Albert, as it happened, was fond of a white rat and would reach out to fondle this creature when given the opportunity. Watson's plan was to create quite the opposite reaction in Albert and, to achieve this, he arranged for two metal plates to be clashed together, just behind Albert's head, whenever the child reached for his 'pet'. Very quickly the anxiety produced by the noise was transferred to the white rat and Albert not only cried but attempted to crawl away when the animal was present. Not entirely surprising of itself, but at least it is an example of how a previously preferred object can become a stimulus to fear and, of course, may well be the model for all abnormal fears. Perhaps less obviously expected were the findings that the fear, once initiated, tended to persist over time (even though no more metal plate clashing took place) and that the fear transferred to objects with some characteristics of the rat, e.g. a ball of cotton wool. This certainly begins to look rather like the 'spread' or 'generalization' of anxiety that we have come to recognize in so many neurotic conditions—the fear may begin in a limited way but begins to become attached to a wide range of situations over a period of time. It may begin, for example, with embarrassment and anxiety about an incident in the Managing Director's office but spread to many other business situations and, of course, will eventually have an entirely mysterious appearance—the logic of the generalization not being apparent by the examination of any one particular example. Certainly Watson was impressed by the way in which a primary cause may be lost to recall, and muses about the future adult Albert lying on the analyst's couch and vainly trying to discover how he came to be afraid of cotton wool.

Watson was a thorough-going environmentalist, believing that heredity and instinct had little or nothing to do with human behaviour. Indeed, he claimed that, given a free hand, he could train any normal child '. . . to become any type of specialist I might select . . . yes, even beggar man and thief, regardless of his talents, penchants, tendencies, abilities, vocations and race of his ancestors'. Although extreme environmentalism is not a corollary of Behaviourism, it is certainly the case that Behaviourists tend to think of the environment as the most important determinant of what we are, although most would accord an important part to hereditary influences of both a specific and a general character, and few would adopt the extreme view espoused by Watson. There are, unfortunately, still a substantial number of sociologists who advance views about the influence of the environment that are ludicrously over-stated and singularly uninformed; such views have, of course, nothing to do with science and merely represent emotionally toned beliefs about the world, as relevant to real knowledge as the Flat Earth Society is to modern navigational systems.

In any event, Behavioural theories became more refined under the influence of many investigators, such as Tolman, Skinner, Guthrie and, very particularly, Hull. Environmental influences were the centre-piece of these investigators and, understandably, this emphasis was upon what the organism could learn and how such learning takes places. They differed among themselves as to the precise way in which learning could be effected but all might be regarded as good Behaviourists in the sense that they were concerned with what could be observed (obviously, overt behaviour in the main) and quantified, and they were experimentalists. Their earnest wish was not so much to deny the complex workings of the central nervous system, but to avoid any complication from mechanisms that could not be directly studied or understood; much better to see how far one could get in predicting and controlling behaviour without reference to poorly understood internal processes.

Essentially, then, Behavioural Psychology has no fixed limits about those things that will be encompassed in its theories and practices; only the stricture that we can measure and 'see' what we are doing. This is, of course, very realistic and practical as, since Watson's days, knowledge of internal processes has increased a great deal so that the modern Behaviourist can come to terms with many areas that were once mysterious or even taboo.

But let us try now to clarify the major difference in approach which gives the shape and feel of the Behaviourist viewpoint and, to do so, a comparison with a very different approach, that of psychotherapy, will be helpful.

We would note for example that while psychotherapy is based upon theories of an intuitive kind, never properly formulated in postulate form, the Behavioural approach bears the hallmarks of science, having properly formulated theories that allow testable deductions to be made.

It would also be apparent that there exists a substantial difference in the background to the collection of basic information; in the case of psychotherapy this has been the clinical case setting—the analytical couch, deprived of careful experimental control. In contrast, the Behaviourist has arrived at his basic data in experimental settings and under conditions where the reliability of such information tends to be much greater.

Furthermore, according to the one view, symptoms are only the external appearances of some deeply hidden 'cause' and merely the flag-waving to indicate distress. The Behaviourist, on the other hand, sees symptoms in their own right as evidence of faulty learning to be corrected through a re-learning process. Indeed, according to this latter view faulty learning is culpable in two senses; firstly, that the individual may have overlearned some behaviour, so that it occurs in contexts where it is unadaptive and irrelevant while, secondly, the individual may appear abnormal because he has failed to acquire some important coping ability. As an example of 'surplus learning' it may be noted that phobias of all kinds belong to this category; anxiety is an appropriate response in some contexts but is judged to be abnormal if it has generalized to quite innocuous stimuli (as in Little Albert). Where the second type of faulty learning is concerned, it is easy to see that problems are created where, for example, the opportunity to acquire social skills has been inadequate or denied. In such cases, of course, it is not only that these skills are missing but there is a 'knock-on' effect in a wide variety of situations. An example of this is Mr B., a successful bank official who had reached a position of considerable responsibility in his organization. Much of this recognition of his worth had been gained as a kind of back-room whizz-kid, but promotion had now pushed him into social situations in which he felt extremely uncomfortable. In these situations he could only cope by confining conversational exchanges to business matters and adopt a contrived severity of manner as a camouflage for his social ineptitude. His banking competence was, of course, unimpaired, but his discomfort was often acute.

Clearly, the objective of therapy should be the provision of new learning opportunities; e.g. to detach anxiety from innocuous events or to teach the missing skills that produce discomfort. At least the direct approach of the Behaviourist argues that this is so. By contrast, the Psychotherapist would wish to examine the problem in historical perspective and search for the 'hidden causes' of problem behaviour, taking no positive action about the aberrant behaviour itself. The Behaviourist would argue that not only would this take a long time but that the unconscious causal mechanism may never be found—and may well not exist.

This brings us to the related question concerning the nature of symptoms. Often the Psychotherapist takes the view that symptoms are tangential to the real problem—almost a camouflage or subterfuge to mislead. Symptoms are, in this view, evidence that the true nature of the problem is being repressed, that is, shut away from conscious recognition. The much simpler view of the Behaviourist is that symptoms are merely the expression of faulty learning and rarely, if ever, mask the 'real' problem.

The two views are sharply contrasted in the case of nocturnal enuresis (bed-wetting). The Psychoanalytic views of such behaviour range from arguing that it represents a substitute for sexual gratification to the contention that it is an expression of resentment against parental authority. The Behaviourist argues simply that bed-wetting is an example of not having learned to achieve bladder control. The Psychoanalyst must, of course, deal with the problem of sexual gratification or with parent–child relationship problems; the Behaviourist must direct his endeavours to teaching bladder control.

In this case focusing directly upon bladder training is highly successful since, in the large majority of cases, a brief period of training leaves the child dry at night.

It can argued that in the case of bed-wetting there is often a fair amount of family friction and discord and that this, surely, suggests that a deeper explanation of causes is likely. The question is, however, that of whether bed-wetting is the primary or the secondary complaint — does the acrimony between parent and older child cause the latter to wet the bed, or could it be that the bed-wetting habit occasions the acrimony? What transpires is that the removal of the symptom by habit training produces a signal improvement in child–parent relationships, and so it seems that the simpler Behavioural view is correct as well as being more successful in dealing with the symptom.

This is likely to be true of many other problem areas and is certainly often seen in the context of sexual difficulties. An individual may claim a lack of sexual feelings and blame this on the clumsiness, insatiable demands, lack of affection, and so on, of the partner. Difficulties multiply for the couple because this one area of functioning is not going well and the resentment of both may affect numerous aspects of their relationship. Where it is apparent to the Behaviour Therapist that the central problem is one of sexual compatibility, he can work on this symptom, hopefully put this matter right, and then sit back to watch other problem areas sort themselves out.

Those who may have been on the receiving end of Psychotherapy or psychoanalysis, or even those who have observed the film or TV depictions of such treatment, will recognize the historically based nature of the therapy, the requirement to look back at early experiences as a way of understanding and treating the symptoms. Rather than a detailed analysis of the current state of play, an individual might be asked to dwell upon his early relationships with his parents, for example. The Behavioural approach, alternatively, looks very particularly at habits or symptoms as they currently exist and may well pay little or no attention to the individual's history.

This sharp difference is carried over into notions which the two approaches entertain towards effecting cures. The psychotherapist tends to the view that the underlying (and largely unconscious) processes must be dealt with before changes are possible, while the Behaviour Therapist inclines to the view that the symptoms alone are the problem, that they are not subserved by complex hidden mechanisms, and that their removal will itself constitute the cure. Each protagonist, of course, carries out a treatment programme consistent with the starting assumptions about how cures are obtained. What you would notice here about the differences in approach are, first, that the time taken in treatment is usually very lengthy for psychotherapy or psychoanalysis (a period of years is not untypical) and comparatively brief for Behavioural treatment; second, that the former methods are far less directive while the latter emphasize the specific goals, behaviours, tasks, and so on that are to be secured; third, that the techniques employed are entirely different. Respecting this third point, for example, it is evident that the interpretation of symptoms, of dreams, and of behaviour is commonly employed in the psychotherapy approach but is accorded no importance in behavioural psychology; in the latter approach the symptoms themselves are the focus of attention, not the thing which they may be alleged to represent or symbolize.

The split between the two viewpoints is very fundamental since it tends to leave very little middle ground to occupy. Indeed, the orthodox psychoanalytic viewpoint would argue that symptomatic treatment is superficial, leaving the 'real' problem yet unresolved and therefore likely to produce a new crop of symptoms as one set is removed. This point has been already touched upon in the context of the treatment of bed-wetting, but it is worth noting that 'symptom substitution' has not appeared to be a hazard of behaviour modification as has been suggested.

Finally, it is pertinent to raise a point of difference between the two approaches in respect of the relationship of therapist to subject. For the Psychotherapist this assumes great importance and, indeed, without the development of a special bond between the parties to treatment, therapy is unsuccessful. For the thoroughgoing Behaviourist the relationship is very much less significant. Indeed, in many cases any re-learning that is necessary could well be accomplished with the aid of a machine or, in other contexts, the re-training could be largely a matter for the individual himself—the therapist's role being confined to merely outlining what is needed and keeping, perhaps, a supervisory eye on the progress made. Good examples of this independence of a therapeutic relationship are not hard to find.

Mr J., a pleasant but rather deferential company solicitor, had found his work suffering considerably because of a problem in his domestic life. The difficulty arose out of a confession, by his wife, that she had been unfaithful on two occasions and, feeling very guilty about her indiscretion, she wanted to rid herself of her bad conscience and assure her husband that there would never be any repetition of such behaviour. Understandably, in the circumstances, Mr J. was profoundly shocked and, for a time, seriously contemplated separation and divorce. However, he made a valiant effort to forgive his wife, even though he found it difficult to forget, and they managed to patch up their relationship.

Unfortunately, Mr J. found it quite impossible to forget about his wife's behaviour and found himself, from time to time, so burdened by the thought that he resorted to questioning her about her disloyalty. This involved going over the smallest detail again and again in, perhaps, a vain attempt to come to terms with the incident or as a means of punishing his wife, as some might argue.

There is clearly fertile soil here for an interpretive approach and considerable opportunities for the intuitions of those wanting to deal in 'relationship problems'. In the meantime, however, Mr J. continues to suffer agonies of mind, his domestic relationship is foundering, and his inefficiency at work has become a matter for concern. For the Behaviourist the problem seems to be starkly simple; since Mrs J. has given up her relationship, regrets it bitterly, and has no intention of letting any future occurrence of this kind disturb their essentially good marriage, then attention must be directed to Mr J.'s obsessive thoughts. In short, if Mr J. could simply stop having these morbid recollections and interrogations, then the marriage might flourish again and he could well manage to resume his old level of work efficiency.

Fortunately, the means of controlling unwanted thoughts are available and the technique is very largely applied by the individual concerned. Lengthy discussions may be unnecessary, a detailed investigation of Mr J.'s childhood development may be irrelevant, and an interpretive inquiry into Mrs J.'s reason for being unfaithful over a period of years may not be required. Rather, a simple, direct approach to the perceived problem could work (and did, in this case).

Yet another example of 'self-help', that of establishing control over physiological processes through biofeedback, is dealt with fully in a later section of this book. Briefly, here is a technique that enables the individual to develop his potential to alter certain physiological conditions that impair effective functioning; the process is one of self-education and the involvement of others is minimal.

In this book we have attempted to bring together our joint experience in dealing with problems of stress by Behavioural techniques. Such problems do not constitute a unique application of the ideas or strategies of behaviour modification since, traditionally, the range of applications has been very broad. Indeed, a unifying feature is found in the idea that adaptation and adjustment is, to a large extent, a matter of learning. Sometimes the individual has learned too well and at other times not well enough, and the analysis of the problem should reveal which of these is the case. Beyond that, the issue is one of selecting an appropriate technique to effect the necessary change. Problems of stress are obviously amenable to the same approach, whether the difficulty has been generated in the work situation or outside it, and whether the primary source of the stress emanates from some external source or from one's own faulty approach. Of course, it may be that such an apparently simple analysis of psychological problems raises doubts in minds attuned to regarding mental mechanisms as infinitely complex and the problems arising from them as being stubborn and unyielding to mere common sense. There is, at least, something to be said for the latter point since common sense appears not to afford adequate protection against stress, but the conclusion that one must therefore have recourse to something unamenable to ordinary understanding must be regarded as quite erroneous. Yet, to the authors of this book, it is revealing how frequently such a view is apparently held by those who, in other contexts, would be insistent upon a hard-headed approach to problems. Hence, one finds a proliferation of methods that have little or no scientific standing readily adopted by individuals or companies on the basis of mere faith.

This may not be so remarkable a matter since there are still many intelligent, perceptive and knowledgeable individuals who (perhaps in a slightly shamefaced way) consult a magazine horoscope or a clairvoyant. Such behaviour, in otherwise rational individuals, perhaps signifies the existence of a problem to which no obvious solution has appeared and, hence, magic must be invoked. Such a conclusion could account for the way in which unproven ideas and practices are warmly embraced in the area of stress control and prevention, such as Est, Actualism, Analytical Tracking, Human Life Styling, Primal Scream, Integral Massage, Neo-Reichian Bodywork, Tai Chi, and many more.

Of course, it may be argued by the committed that those exposed to these methods can show a surprising degree of change—at least outwardly; as Cyra McFadden's fictional character puts it 'Est just changed my whole life. I never knew before what a total shit I was.'

Our point is that the Behavioural approach commends itself as having a scientific basis; its ideas and methods derive from laboratory experiment and they are amenable to test and disproof. Furthermore, the empirical evidence is that they work well in practical situations. As we have already indicated, there are gaps in knowledge and some constraints on the usefulness of such an approach, but at least we have a good idea what these are.

First, it should be apparent to us all that in spite of Watson's rash assertions silk purses are not made from sow's ears. We do have different constitutions and the factors underlying such differences can affect the rate of our learning as well as the very capacity to change. The same stressors do not affect everyone in the same way; some of us are more vulnerable or susceptible by our very nature and this will of course affect what happens. Some individuals probably should not occupy positions where there are a multitude of stressors, a conclusion not easy to accept, particularly where those individuals have very considerable talents and a matching ambition to be successful. It is possible to identify such individuals and to advise accordingly respecting their existing capacity to tolerate a stressful existence; we find it surprising that few companies make such inquiries before choosing an individual who will assume great responsibilities, a stressful existence and a salary to match.

On the other hand, there are many who have a degree of vulnerability that could be usefully tempered by teaching appropriate coping skills in a prophylactic way. Yet others, currently exposed to stressors that are proving burdensome, might well be advised to acquire an amelioration or even immunity by taking appropriate action.

This book is directed to these latter groups. Our intention is to outline some simple behavioural strategies of established value to an interested readership. In this way we hope to create an appropriate understanding of the application of psychological science to an important human problem area.

Chapter 3

Identification of Stressors: Behavioural Analysis

Many problems can arise in relation to the stressors to which we are exposed, and it is important that we are able to identify these problems accurately, and specify precisely the changes we wish to make. The behavioural approach emphasizes careful delineation and measurement of all aspects of the problem. The use of behavioural analysis of an individual's problems arose in the clinical field, largely as a reaction against what was seen to be the inadequacies of existing diagnostic systems and psychoanalytic formulation. In particular Kanfer and Saslow (1969) did much to bring this approach to the attention of clinicians, and we shall consider their behavioural analytic approach in some detail.

The crux of the approach is to specify as precisely as possible the preceding events and environmental factors which control the problem behaviour. Lindsley (1964) has described the components which might be thought necessary for a full behavioural analysis as (1) the stimulus, (2) the response, (3) the contingency-related conditions and (4) the consequences of the behaviour; to this Kanfer and Saslow added (5) the biological state of the person.

The analysis must include all events which might be relevant and not merely psychological events, that is biological, social and economic events must all be considered. The purpose of the analysis is to identify the problems and, by precisely studying the relevant factors surrounding the problem, to come up with an effective strategy to combat that particular difficulty. It may often be the case that there is no necessity to consider changing the individual but that it is necessary to restructure his environment in some way, perhaps by changing the physical environment or by changing the behaviour of significant other people in that individual's environment. An example of the need for some simple environmental change was shown in the case of a senior Civil Servant who had suffered a tension reaction which had been expressed by excruciating chest pain which had occurred at precisely 4 o'clock in the afternoon, the subject having been looking at his large office clock at the exact time the attack occurred. At first it was assumed that the Civil Servant had suffered a heart attack, but it rapidly became apparent that this was not the case. However, the poor chap returned to work and found that he continued to suffer attacks every afternoon at 4 o'clock. Of course, treatment involved a complex package including determining the causes of the stress reaction, but an important component was the removal of the large wall clock!

In the final chapter there are some checklists which might provide a first approximation to the identification of problem behaviours. Once this stage has been reached it is then necessary to determine specific details of the problem.

Kanfer and Saslow recommend viewing behaviour in terms of:

(a) behavioural excesses;
(b) behavioural deficits;
(c) behavioural assets.

(a) BEHAVIOURAL EXCESSES

A behaviour may become a problem because it is excessive in terms of:

(1) frequency;
(2) intensity;
(3) duration;
(4) the behaviour is not normally sanctioned in that social setting at all.

The need for very frequent coffee breaks could be a problem subsumed under (1). Anger in response to trivial situations could be an example of (2), a continued preoccupation with checking reports or typescripts for accuracy could be (3), and (4) would include such behaviours as sexual exhibitionism or possibly arriving at the office in the morning already under the influence of alcohol.

(b) BEHAVIOURAL DEFICITS

A deficit would be indicated when a behaviour fails to occur:

(1) with sufficient frequency;
(2) with adequate intensity;

(3)   with appropriate form;
(4)   under socially expected conditions.

Examples would be shyness resulting in a deficit in social behaviours of various sorts, a lack of emotional warmth, sexual performance problems such as impotence or frigidity, writer's cramp which would show a deficit in writing production but an excess in muscle tension.

(c) BEHAVIOURAL ASSETS

These are non-problem behaviours. It is necessary to take stock of all the strengths an individual might have; what he excels at. Any area of his life might well be useful in helping to produce beneficial change, any skill or attribute or talent.

The first stage of analysis is therefore the identification of the problem. This should be tied down to some clear-cut behavioural description. For instance, if an executive complains of 'underachievement' it is first necessary to tie this down to specifics: what work function does he consider he is underachieving in? What is his expectation for this function? The next stage is to assign the problems, as they are identified to the categories of excesses, deficits, et cetera. The next stage is to determine who regards these behaviours as a problem? Is it the executive himself, his superiors, his subordinates, his family?

The next point to consider is the consequences the problem has for the individual and others around him. Perspectives may vary on this of course. An executive who habitually takes his work home, closets himself in his study for 4 hours each evening in order to complete tasks for the following day may be regarded as a paragon by his boss, but his wife and family could have very different views! At this stage it is also necessary to consider what consequences removal of the problem would have for the individual and those around him. If removal of one undesirable behaviour is followed by the substitution of another then there may be no gain. If our busy executive was persuaded to reorganize his work-load so that he did not need to take work home, and if he now used the time gained to spend in excessive drinking, his family might well feel that little had been accomplished. It is necessary to plan at an early stage how one's lifestyle can be reshaped.

It is now necessary to consider in detail the circumstances in which the problem behaviours occur. It is usually helpful at this stage for the subject to engage in self-monitoring to try to pinpoint the precise conditions under which the problem occurs. For example, time of day, place, et cetera. If a person had a weight problem it would usually be most illuminating for them to make an accurate note of what, when and where they ate. The conditions may be social or vocational, or biological. A female data processor may find that she makes many more errors at the premenstrual phase of her cycle.

What satisfaction does the individual derive from his problem behaviour? What new satisfations might he gain if this behaviour were changed. It is necessary to carefully consider the profit and loss, both to the individual and those around him, and to consider how the individual might continue with his life if there was no change in his problem behaviour. A basic tenet of the behavioural approach, which underlies the above points, is that behaviour is maintained. The problem is not viewed as having arisen from some traumatic event in early childhood, possibly submerged for several years, only to arise in adulthood having been fuelled by some mysterious internal source of energy. The behavioural approach emphasizes that there is continued support for the behaviour operating in the present. If powerful sources of reinforcement for the problem behaviour are not defined then change is impossible.

Motivational analysis

(a) First one must determine how much the individual values the various incentives and rewards which are available to him. There are available some checklists covering common incentives but thinking systematically about the topic will soon produce a list which applies to oneself. The value one assigns to any particular incentive can be determined by the price one is willing to pay for it, in terms of expenditure of time, effort, physical discomfort, et cetera. The list of possible reinforcers is very wide and would include, for example, money, good health, recognition and approval from one's superiors, friendship and approval from one's peers, approval from one's subordinates, social approval, work satisfaction, sports achievement, free time, sexual satisfaction, control over others, et cetera.

(b) What is the past history of success with each particular reinforcer? Does the individual frequently achieve success in acquiring these incentives? What expectations of success or failure does he have? Under what precise conditions has success or failure resulted in relation to each of these incentives?

(c) Under what conditions, specified in precise detail, does the individual strive for each incentive. The conditions considered should cover the whole range applicable to the individual, that is cover work and home and social situations, biological states, etc. It is a commonplace observation that the goals sought by a person might change drastically when he has had a few drinks; a petty office tyrant may become a Don Juan at the office party!

(d) Is there any discrepancy between the stated goals of a person and his actual behaviour? This normally requires the assistance of somebody able to give an objective external audit of the person's behaviour. Few of us have the necessary objectivity to be able to determine that there is a great discrepancy between what we say are our goals, and what observation of our behaviour suggests is actually our goals. Most people are capable of some degree of self-deception. If there is an observable discrepancy how does this affect the goals of any programme aimed to promote change?

(e) Who has the most effective control over the person's behaviour, which person or group of people, and under what conditions?

(f) Does the person understand the relationship of reinforcement contingencies to his own behaviour, or does he feel that reinforcement is just a matter of chance events? That is, does he attribute a major role to random factors, good luck or bad luck, fate, 'superstitious' behaviour, et cetera. Does he believe that he can influence events, that he is master of his own fate; does he have an 'internal' or 'external' locus of control? The concept of locus of control is discussed further in the chapter on biofeedback since it is of direct relevance to the control of physiological behaviour.

(g) What are the major punishing and aversive events in the individual's life? These should be considered both in relation to his present-day life and also his fears for the future. Is he most concerned with social disapproval, for example; failing to produce a report on time may elicit criticism from his boss? On the other hand the most aversive event could be the internal sensations resulting from the physiological component of the stress response, summoning up fears of a serious illness. What consequence does he fear and dread, what outcome or event is he at most pains to avoid?

(h) Would a programme aimed at change have the requirement that the individual would have to give up some current satisfaction which is associated with the present problem. For example the known propensity for 'migraine' headaches might excuse a person from having to perform some tedious duty, which in reality should be part of his responsibilities. Or an illness might serve to justify an individual fulfilling the expectations both he and others once entertained for him.

(i) Finally, what incentives of known reinforcing value might be used in a programme aimed at change? By what means, under what conditions, in what circumstances can positive contingencies be arranged to follow from the new desired behaviour, to replace the aversive consequences which used to result from these circumstances?

Developmental analysis

(a) Biological factors.

It is necessary to consider the biological status of the person in relation to both his problems and his goals. Does he have physical handicaps such as poor eyesight, colour blindness, defective hearing, speech defect, et cetera? Are these remediable? Does he have some residual disability from a prior illness, for example a stroke leaving a slight degree of paralysis, a heart attack leaving an intense preoccupation with vulnerability, etc. What limitations do these factors impose? For example the necessity to receive renal dialysis three times per week might greatly restrict mobility. Under what conditions and to what extent do these biological factors maintain problem behaviours? For example a fear of exertion following a heart attack might lead to a restriction in sexual activity within a marriage, leading to marital problems, guilt and despondency because of the marital problems, resulting in diminished work output leading to further guilt and so on in a downward spiral. It is very important in these circumstances to determine how far it might be possible to change the individual's self-limiting concepts about his restrictions, and how far the biological constraints set real limits on the degree of change possible. It is also necessary to consider the history of the biological limitations, how they arose, what effects they have had on the individual and on the perception of himself by himself and others. What has been done about these problems in the past, et cetera.

(b) Sociological factors

A close definition of the individual's sociocultural background is required. This would consider such factors as social class, rural versus urban environment, educational background, religious affiliation. How congruent is the individual's behaviour and attitudes with his socio-cultural background?

Is the problem behaviour related to changes in the sociocultural background. If this is the case then what were the circumstances surrounding the changes, who did they involve (i.e. family, et cetera)? Are the changes permanent or temporary? Do the changes have consequences for the subject and his immediate family? For example rapid upward social mobility due to promotion for an able executive may on occasion have serious effects on his wife and family because of the expectation that they now need to conform to a new set of social mores and pressures, particularly if the executive has been promoted from the shop floor and will now be socially interacting with a set of people with different educational backgrounds.

As we have seen in Chapter 1, a further factor may be the geographical mobility often expected from executives nowadays. An executive's wife, largely housebound because of young children, may find herself suddenly uprooted from all her social support facilities, family, friends, et cetera. She might find it very difficult to re-establish links in her new environment, and thus be deprived of many of the reinforcers she previously enjoyed. Her husband, faced with the problems of adjusting to a new working environment and new set of personalities, is thus confronted by a wife manifesting all the symptoms of a depressive reaction.

If there have been changes, it is important to determine the individual's attitudes towards the changes, and discover what attributions he makes about the changes. Who does he consider responsible for the changes? Again, does he attribute the changes to himself, or others, or the machinations of a malign fate? Are the individual's roles in the various social settings in which he functions congruent, or is there dissonance and conflict? For example, value systems acquired earlier in the person's life may now be in conflict with the social demands of his present role. Loss of earning power following redundancy, and re-employment at a lower level than previously, may also produce dramatic conflict between the expectations of the individual and his family and the new hard reality. If such role conflict does exist then it is necessary to demonstrate that it is of some significance in terms of the problem behaviour.

Finally, the analysis will indicate whether the problem behaviour manifests itself in all or only some of the social settings encountered by the individual.

(c) Behavioural factors

The behavioural patterns of the individual should be scrutinized in order to determine whether any changes had occurred in his behaviour in relation to the prevailing social or developmental norms at that time. If changes had occurred what was the nature of these changes? What were the conditions operating when these changes first became apparent? What factors can be identified which seem to be relevant to these changes, what biological or social events appear relevant? What characteristics did the changes have, i.e. did new behaviours emerge, or was there a change in the frequency, duration or intensity of a previously established behaviour?

Analysis of self-control

Since the individual will probably not manifest his problem behaviour in all situations it is necessary to establish in which situations he can control his problem behaviour and discover how he achieves such control. What has been the effect of any aversive consequences which have occurred in the past—for example, dismissal, fines or prison sentences, ostracism, et cetera? A case in point would be to discover if a drunk-driving conviction produced any change in the excessive drinking habit of an executive. Did these events produce any changes in the individual's self-control behaviour? Has the individual learned any strategies for avoiding situations which are conducive to his problem behaviour? How consistent is his self-description of his self-control compared to the descriptions of others? How much supervision would be required to supplement the individual's efforts at self-control?

Analysis of social relationships

The purpose of this analysis is to determine who are the most significant people in the individual's present social environment. To whom is he most responsive, to whom is he most antagonistic, who is most likely to provoke his problem behaviours, is there any discernible pattern to this? For example, a person may behave in a highly socially inhibited manner with anybody he perceives to be his social superior and behave differently with anybody else. Or some young men find it difficult to interact with the opposite sex but can behave perfectly normally when in the company of other males. What are the potent reinforcers being applied between people in the individual's background? What are the mutual expectations of the individual and significant others, and finally can these significant others play a part in the retraining of his problem behaviour?

Analysis of the social–cultural–physical environment

Finally it is necessary to determine what are the norms in the subject's background environment for the problem behaviour. Are there any major differences in the acceptability or otherwise of his behaviours in the various social backgrounds in which he interacts. For example, the norms for drinking behaviour might be very different for his work colleagues than for the members of a rugby club at which he spends a great deal of his leisure time. Are there any limitations which reduce his opportunity for reinforcement in any of the various backgrounds, et cetera.

This outline should give an indication of what is required from an effective behavioural analysis of any problem behaviour. Throughout the emphasis is upon seeking to define the behaviour in terms of clear behavioural referents, rather than upon vague and nebulous constructs. It is not very helpful for a person to complain of suffering from 'unhappiness'. We would wish to know much more about it, how it is expressed, what the behavioural consequences are for being unhappy, under what conditions does it arise and under what conditions does it dissipate, et cetera. An effective behavioural analysis allows one not only to determine precisely what the problem is, but also to formulate a strategy for changing the behaviour and also to know what limitations — physical, biological, social, or sociological — there might be, in order to arrive at realistic goals and expectations. Since clear-cut goals can be formulted in behavioural terms, it follows that this process lends itself very readily to monitoring and measurement of change.

It should be clear from the foregoing that the sources of information required for a behavioural analysis of a problem behaviour go far beyond merely verbal report from the individual. Observation of the behaviour within the naturalistic environment might be required, the observations of significant others would obviously be of value, the use of video might be required, role-play of particular interactions might produce invaluable information, et cetera. To clarify the picture it will be helpful to look at the possibilities for the analysis of a particular type of problem, and we commence by considering the behavioural analysis of anxiety.

BEHAVIOURAL ANALYSIS OF ANXIETY AND FEAR

Anxiety and fear are, in fact, merely labels for a response complex consisting of three components. There is the verbal report of the mental experience of anxiety and apprehension; there is the physiological experience which stems from arousal of the sympathetic branch of the autonomic nervous system, resulting in such phenomena as sweating palms, trembling, muscle tension, acceleration of heart rate, cessation of digestive processes, et cetera. The third component is behavioural effects such as avoidance and performance inefficiency. People usually show a reactivity in all three components but there are circumstances in which the components may be poorly correlated and may change at different rates.

If a person complains of anxiety what does this mean? Does he or she experience panic, palpitations, dizziness? How does he react to these experiences, does he avoid or confront situations which elicit these experiences? What are the precise situational, cognitive or internal proprioceptive stimuli that are associated with anxiety reactions of varying intensity? In addition to self-report measures, therapists may employ such techniques as imagery or role-playing. Imagery techniques can be useful in helping clients to make discriminations which might be difficult under normal consulting-room conditions. In this technique the client is asked to close his eyes and vividly imagine some specific past or future situation as if he were really there. He is then asked questions about aspects of the imagined stimulus situation or his thoughts while in that situation, or asked to define his probable behaviour in that situation.

Role-playing can be useful in helping a client delineate specific problems associated with particular situations involving interpersonal performance, for example initiating a conversation with an eligible female.

SELF-REPORT MEASURES

There has been a tendency for workers in the behavioural tradition to rather underplay the importance of self-report measures. Emphasis was placed upon the development of physiological and behavioural methods as it was expected that these measures might have greater validity and reliability than self-report measures. However, it has become apparent that observational and physiological methods also have interpretive problems and are subject to artifact and biases.

Self-report measures can be used to assess cognitive, behavioural and physiological indices of anxiety. Self-report measures of cognitive anxiety often correlate very poorly with measures of overt, fearful behaviour, but it is becoming increasingly clear that these two aspects of anxiety often proceed at very different rates. There are a number of studies, however, which show a good correlation between self-reports and measures of easily discriminable events, e.g. number of occasions a person has made a date with a member of the opposite sex.

Because of the poor correlation often found between cognitive anxiety and behavioural or physiological measures it follows that under certain conditions the correlation will be poor even if the self-report measure is perfectly valid. There have been theoretical objections raised to self-report measures along the lines that they are open to wilful distortion on the part of the client, or rely heavily on the client's ability to make verbal discriminations which break down under certain conditions, e.g. drugs, fatigue, extreme stress reactions. This merely indicates the inappropriateness of this form of measure in certain situations.

As to the problem of deliberate distortion on the part of the client, there is little evidence at the present time to indicate to what extent this may be a problem, or whether self-report measures are any more vulnerable in that respect than other measures, such as a behavioural approach measure.

There are in existence several standardized self-report measures, such as the Fear Survey Schedule developed by Wolpe and Lang (1964), although many variants exist. Typically these instruments ask the client to rate his anxiety on a five-point scale in relation to a wide variety of experiences and situations, such as feeling pain in the chest, being criticized, being rejected, et cetera. The major problem with this approach is that the items are divorced from specific situations and these measures are only useful as a first approximation to 'home in' on an area of difficulty. The checklists in the final chapter again should be used in this fashion rather than being regarded as providing definitive information.

Since the major concern of anybody seeking help to reduce anxiety is to reach a state where they actually feel that their anxiety has diminished, it follows that a measure of cognitive anxiety is of considerable importance. One such measure is the 'Fear Thermometer'; this is a scale from 1 to 100 with 1 indicating 'absolute calm' and 100 indicating 'absolute terror'. The client has to indicate where they are on this scale at any particular time. Sometimes a 10-point scale is used, but the principle is the same.

There are a number of measures which have been developed for specific fears, such as public-speaking, test-anxiety, et cetera. These are usually questionnaires arranged to tap the three components of anxiety, i.e. cognitive, behavioural and physiological. These appear to be of some use in initial screening and as an adjunctive measure during retraining.

Self-monitoring is being used increasingly in the area of self-control. Clients are asked to keep written records of easily discriminable events, number of cigarettes smoked in particular situations, food or alcohol consumed, et cetera. The technique has shown considerable promise in the self-control area, but has been relatively little applied to anxiety measurement, although it would appear to have considerable potential application in this area. It is, however, probable that most people find self-monitoring somewhat aversive, and it is important to build into the procedure some reinforcer of sufficient value as to overcome the aversive quality of the procedure.

BEHAVIOURAL OBSERVATION

The direct observation of the client's behaviour in the presence of anxiety-eliciting stimuli is central to the behavioural approach to assessment. Such techniques have ranged from unobtrusive observation in the natural environment to direct observation of the client's behaviour on some standardized test in the clinic or laboratory. Lang and Lazovick introduced the first behavioural approach test (BAT) in 1963 as a measure of the fear of snakes. Subjects were asked to approach as close as they could to a caged snake and if possible to handle the snake. Measurements were taken before and after treatment. The distance that the subject was able to reach was used as a measure, and it was then possible to quantify improvement in terms of decrease in distance from the snake.

Since 1963 there have been hundreds of studies involving BATs as a measure in a wide variety of fear stimuli. However, it is now apparent that there are a number of factors producing the possibility of bias on this test. There is the 'demand' characteristics of the situation, subjects being aware that they are expected to do better after treatment than before and being unwilling to disappoint the therapist. This is the well known 'Hello–Goodbye' effect of orthodox psychotherapy.

It is also apparent that BAT performance is sensitive to various aspects of the instructions given, and also the test, although incorporating a feared object, is nevertheless administered in a safe environment. All these effects are likely to produce some bias when compared to how the subject might perform in the real environment, and there is some experimental evidence to support this.

ROLE-PLAYING TESTS

Clients are asked to role-play responses to pre-recorded social stimuli presented on audio or video tape. This technique has been used to assess deficits in assertive behaviour and can easily be adapted to situations of central importance to the manager's role, for example to some industrial bargaining situation. During the role-play the client's responses can be evaluated along a variety of dimensions, interpersonal behaviours such as eye-contact, variables such as posture, speech latency and loudness, physiological measures are also easily obtainable, and so on. A major advantage is the ease with which a wide variety of anxiety-provoking situations may be presented. The drawback, of course, lies in the fact that this is not a situation arising in the natural environment and therefore may not elicit the full anxiety response. Nevertheless, the method is useful for training as well as measurement purposes.

INTERPERSONAL PERFORMANCE TEST

This is a technique which has been used, for example by Paul in 1966, to measure public-speaking anxiety. The test involved having subjects give a short speech before a small audience while trained observers rated the occurrence of visible aspects of anxiety. This technique has since been modified to assess anxiety produced by other stimuli, for example having male subjects try to interact with an unresponsive female in an attempt to create a favourable impression. A good deal of further research is required to ensure adequate knowledge of this technique, but certainly the technique offers promise.

Finally, there is the possibility of observation in the natural environment. This poses several problems. If the subject is aware of being observed then there is the question of reactivity; that is that the subject's behaviour may be different under this condition than if he were unaware of being observed. If the observation is unobtrusive then there are practical limits on the type of situation that can be encompassed by the technique, and some important ethical difficulties are also raised. It is, of course, possible with current advances in technology to equip subjects with physiological recording equipment and monitor these responses in the natural environment. This can be done directly, using telemetric techniques—that is using a radio transmitter to transmit information over some distance, or the information can be stored on tape and analysed later. This can be a useful technique in some cases, but we have already indicated that there are problems produced by the fact that the three components of anxiety do not change in a synchronous manner. The bulk of the evidence currently available suggests that such asynchronies disappear over time and that it is the behavioural component which is often the first to change; the other components following later.

Once an anxiety response has been identified it is, of course, necessary to follow the fully detailed analysis as suggested by Kanfer and Saslow. Although we have dealt at some length with anxiety, similar considerations would apply in the behavioural analysis of any negative emotion or problem behaviour. To crystallize the essential point of behavioural analysis, one would say that this is the recognition that problem behaviours occur in specific contexts and it is important to identify *all* relevant aspects of the contextual relationship.

Chapter 4
Relaxation Techniques in the Control of Tension

INTRODUCTION

We have seen in an earlier chapter that the stressors encountered in the modern world produce states of muscular overtension which, in turn, can disrupt the adaptive functioning of various bodily systems. The high incidence of tension disorders well attests to the fact that many people do not have adequate coping skills to deal with the stressful reactions of everyday life. One skill to control overtension, which most people can acquire, is progressive relaxation.

What do we mean by terms such as tension and relaxation? To the layman relaxation can mean anything from engaging in sporting activities, watching television, to going on a holiday. In like manner, tension can refer to hostile atmospheres, aversive feelings within the individual, et cetera. However, from a scientific point of view, relaxation refers to the lengthening of skeletal muscle fibres, while tension refers to the contraction or shortening of muscle fibres.

There are some 620 skeletal muscles in the human body. These are also referred to as the voluntary muscles as we can exercise conscious, voluntary control over them. Skeletal muscles are composed of bundles of parallel fibres; each of the fibres is made up of large numbers of slim filaments which contract and expand. When thousands of these work in co-ordination the muscle contracts. During muscular contraction glycogen, a form of sugar, is broken down, heat is produced and fatigue products — mostly lactic acid — are formed. The products are cleared away in the blood stream, especially when the muscles are relaxed. However, if the muscles are held in a state of contraction for a long interval, the circulation is impeded and the fatigue products build up rapidly. This accumulation leads to cramp-like spasms resulting in aches and pains in the neck and shoulder muscles, backaches and headaches, et cetera.

The task of learning to thoroughly relax groups of muscles is not always an easy one. The habit of muscular tension may be acquired over a large number of years. Clearly, if there have been many years of injudicious use of the muscles leading to chronic malfunctioning of various bodily processes, it seems reasonable that it will take some time to re-educate them. Most people, given regular practice, can reverse long-standing, maladaptive, muscular habits.

HISTORICAL ASPECTS OF PROGRESSIVE RELAXATION TRAINING

It is generally recognized that there are two distinct phases in the history of relaxation training.

The first phase began with the work of Dr Edmund Jacobson, the recognized pioneer in the field of relaxation therapy. His investigations began in 1908 in the laboratory at Harvard University. Further studies were carried out in Chicago, at the University there, and at the Laboratory for Clinical Physiology. Jacobson's results appeared in scientific journals and in 1938 he published a book entitled *Progressive Relaxation*. From his knowledge acquired by electronically monitoring the activity of nervous and muscular systems he established an important principle: relaxation is the direct physiological opposite of tension or excitement; it is the absence of nerve muscle impulses. Jacobson trained his clients to systematically contract and relax groups of muscles; by having them pay attention to, and discriminate, the subsequent sensations of tension and relaxation they were able to almost totally eliminate muscular tension and to experience feelings of profound relaxation. However, a major drawback of Jacobson's method was that it required extensive training over some considerable period of time.

Joseph Wolpe, currently Professor of Psychiatry at Temple University and the Eastern Pennsylvania Psychiatric Institute, was instrumental in developing the second phase of relaxation methods. He produced experimental neuroses in cats by evoking anxiety brought about by placing them in a restricted environment and administering harmless, but unpleasant, electric shocks. The anxiety persisted and resulted in inhibition of adaptive functions; for example, if the cat was starved for 48 hours and was then placed in the experimental cage with pellets of fresh meat, it refused to eat. Wolpe found that the fears generalized—the animals showed strong anxiety on the floor of the laboratory and less so in other rooms according to the degree of likeness to the laboratory. Wolpe compared these patterns of behaviour with human neurotic patterns—the latter he believed to be also persistent and to exhibit generalization; thus, in humans, there could be an inhibition of adaptive functions; for example, failure to eat (anorexia nervosa), impaired social activities, sexual inadequacies, et cetera. In considering the problem of the neuroses in the cats, Wolpe reasoned that, if the anxiety could be inhibited by feeding, then food, made available under conditions in which the anxiety was much weaker, might inhibit the anxiety. He achieved this goal by first feeding the cats in rooms which were unlike the experimental room; then, in a gradual manner, he had them eat in rooms resembling the laboratory; finally he had them eat in the experimental cage in the laboratory. Using similar reasoning Wolpe realized that, in humans, deep relaxation could be used to inhibit anxiety evoked by fear-arousing stimuli. Wolpe had arrived at much the same conclusion as Jacobson: the autonomic effects accompanying deep relaxation are diametrically opposed to those characteristic of anxiety. Because of the prohibitive amount of time required for Jacobsonian relaxation training, Wolpe modified and developed the training programme. This more efficient relaxation programme consisted of half-a-dozen training sessions with home practice between the sessions. Further developments in relaxation methods have taken place since Wolpe modified the training procedures.

BENEFITS OF DEEP RELAXATION

As relaxation is incompatible with tension, the potential advantages of relaxation are numerous. Burns (1981) has listed a number of the advantages, some of which are briefly summarized below:

(1) The general effects of stress may be dealt with more competently, leading to an ability to avoid overreacting.
(2) Stress-related problems such as hypertension, tension headaches, insomnia, et cetera, may be eliminated or ameliorated.
(3) Anxiety levels may be significantly reduced. There is evidence to show that individuals with high levels of anxiety will demonstrate the greatest positive physiological effect of relaxation training.
(4) Preventive aspects of relaxation training are important, both in reducing the likelihood of the onset of stress-related disorders and in the control of anticipatory anxiety before anxiety-provoking

situations, such as an important board meeting, a significant interview, et cetera.

(5) Research demonstrates that certain behaviours are likely to occur more frequently during periods of stress; thus there may be an increase in the number of cigarettes smoked, in alcohol consumption, drug intake (tranquillizers and sedatives), compulsive overeating, et cetera. Relaxation should help to diminish the need to depend on such stress inhibitors. It has the advantage of having few unpleasant side-effects.

(6) Overall improvement in performance of vocational, social and physical skills may occur as a result of reduced levels of tension.

(7) Fatigue, due to prolonged mental activity and/or physical exercise may be overcome more rapidly by using relaxation skills.

(8) Self-awareness of one's physiological state may be increased as a result of relaxation training; this enables the individual to use his relaxation skills at the onset of psychophysiological arousal, et cetera.

(9) Relaxation can be an aid to recovery after certain illnesses and surgery. There is also evidence that it can raise the threshold of tolerance to pain.

(10) An important psychological consequence of relaxation is that the individual's level of self-esteem and self-assuredness is likely to be increased as a result of much-improved control of stress reactions.

(11) Interpersonal relationships may expect to improve. During high levels of tension, cognitive distortions resulting in the adoption of untenable positions are more likely to arise. The relaxed person in difficult interpersonal situations will think more rationally. Also, a relaxed person, through modelling processes, may have a notable calming effect on an emotionally upset person.

POINTS TO BEAR IN MIND ABOUT RELAXATION TRAINING

(1) Relaxation is a self-control method. Evidence suggests that substantial improvement will occur only if the individual realizes that relaxation is an active coping skill to be practised and applied to daily life. Increased control of one's reactions is an important outcome reported by individuals who have successfully completed training. Thus, relaxation involves the active participation of individuals in modifying their responses to stressful events. In

addition to the feeling of control, the individuals develop a feeling of having begun to assume responsibility for the management of their own lives and their own health.

(2) Paradoxically, perhaps, although relaxation is an active process, the individual gains control over himself by letting go. Stressful situations generally result in tightening the reins of control. As Benson (1975) notes, an important component of the relaxation response is a passive, 'letting it happen' attitude of mind.

(3) If it is accepted that learning to relax involves learning a skill, like learning a new sport, then it follows that disciplined, regular practice is essential. Research evidence suggests that greater gains will be made when relaxation is practised under these conditions. During the basic stage relaxation should be practised for at least 30 minutes each day; during the intermediate and advanced stages, it should be practised for 15/20 minutes. Thereafter the skill should be maintained by practising for 15/20 minutes, two or three times each week although the number of sessions will depend on the individual and the stressors encountered in everyday life.

(4) It needs to be borne in mind that relaxation training is one method, albeit an important one, amongst many which may be used in controlling tension. Thus relaxation may, in some cases, be seen as but a part of a therapeutic programme which might also include cognitive restructuring, desensitization, biofeedback, et cetera.

(5) During relaxation there is a lowering of tension level and a slowing down of bodily processes; these physical effects are frequently accompanied by a change in the direction of thought processes — there may be a feeling of calmness and a less critical or demanding attitude. In this state there is sometimes a tendency to drift off to sleep. This should be resisted unless relaxation is being used specifically to overcome a problem of insomnia. The goal of training is to be deeply relaxed while remaining wide awake.

(6) The setting where the relaxation is to take place is of some consequence. Clearly it will be difficult to learn to relax in an environment with extraneous noise. Although the eyes should be kept closed during relaxation the process may be facilitated if the illumination is kept low. Advice is often sought as to whether it would be best to relax on a chair or on a bed. Our experience suggests that reclining chairs, such as the Parker Knoll, are ideal as their use may help to facilitate the transfer of relaxation to life

situations. However, any easy chair with arms will suffice; the important matter is to ensure that the individual is sitting or reclining comfortably, thus keeping muscular tension to a minimum. It is best to inform household members that a relaxation training session is in progress so that the possibility of being disturbed is minimized.

(7) As has been seen, high levels of tension can lead to rigid control. The overtense individual may have developed a pathological overawareness of anxiety-producing internal and external cues. Thus, he may engage in excessive monitoring of his physiological state. Homing in on such feelings, without bringing into play adequate coping skills, tends to reinforce and strengthen the feelings, thereby confirming the disability. Such an individual may have fears of losing control while learning to relax; this may manifest itself by the individual being able to relax to a certain stage and being unable to proceed beyong it. In such a case it is important that a rationale is given for the difficulty; training sessions may be short to begin with. With perseverance this problem can usually be overcome. Bear in mind that the individual always remains in final control and may abort the session if too much uneasiness is experienced.

(8) While the muscles are beginning to unwind a number of unusual feelings may be experienced — feelings such as heaviness in parts of the body, floating in the air, tingling sensations, sudden muscular contractions ('electric shocks'), et cetera. Such feelings are frequently reported and are no cause for concern. Should they interfere with the relaxation process they may be effectively overcome by opening the eyes, by breathing somewhat more deeply and by slowly contracting the muscles throughout the body. Relaxation training may then be recommenced.

(9) Concentration is a problem about which most people make comment. Clearly it is not possible to focus one's mind on relaxation for a long period of time. Accordingly, it is important to re-concentrate on relaxation as soon as possible after the intruding thoughts have been monitored. Under no circumstances should the individual dwell on his anxieties while attempting to relax!

(10) When reading the instructions for the relaxation procedures it will be observed that various groups of muscles are systematically tensed and relaxed; the tension should be released immediately and not be allowed to dissipate slowly.

(11) A valuable aspect of the relaxation training process is to have the individual discriminate the feelings of tension and relaxation in his muscles. Thus, while the muscles are tensed or relaxed the appropriate feelings should be monitored. In everyday life, as tension builds up by an insidious process over a period of time, except during acute phases, the individual may not recognize that he is tense. He may have developed the ability to 'block out' signs of bodily tension; increased self-awareness enables him to utilize his skills in response to stressful life situations.

(12) After a group of muscles has been completely relaxed there is advantage in not moving that group although, if discomfort is experienced, the individual may feel free to move his position.

(13) A goal of relaxation is to remove excessive stress which may be interfering with the optimal functioning of the individual. The goal is not to attain a complete absence of stress or tension; even if the extinction of all signs of anxiety were possible it would be maladaptive as some level of tension is necessary for our welfare and for aiding performance.

(14) During relaxation training try to breathe in and out normally, except while contracting the muscle groups; when contracting the muscles breathe in, hold the breath, relax the muscle group exhaling at the same time; then resume normal breathing. Just prior to releasing the tension say the word 'Relax' or 'Calm' to yourself.

(15) The relaxation training session should always end by tensing all the groups of muscles and by breathing in and out more deeply *before* arising from the chair.

(16) A question frequently asked is 'When is the best time to relax?' There are no hard and fast rules about this and it depends on personal circumstances; for the person at business, perhaps on his arrival home before having his meal might be an ideal time: the housewife may find the early afternoon the best time to relax. However, some trainers do recommend that relaxation should not normally be carried out within an hour of going to bed as there is an increased likelihood of drifting off to sleep.

(17) A more important issue than the timing of the relaxation session is one concerning the availability of an adequate period in which to relax. The high-powered businessman may complain that he cannot find 20 minutes per day to relax. Such a lifestyle merely demonstrates the need for such a period. Even Churchill, while

Prime Minister, during the Second World War, always took time off to relax.

(18) Recognize that the ability to relax can vary on a day-to-day basis. Thus on some days it may be possible to attain very deep levels of relaxation: on other occasions the depth may be minimal. These fluctuations may be due to the current physiological state of the body (this can include pre-menstrual tension and sleep deprivation), excess anxieties, work overload, et cetera.

(19) Most people can learn to accurately recognize the feelings associated with relaxation — sensations of heaviness, particularly in the limbs, a regular pattern of breathing, no signs of muscular tension, especially in the forehead, neck or stomach muscles, a feeling of calmness, tranquillity and peacefulness, et cetera. Occasionally, an individual may report that, whereas he is generally very relaxed, he had difficulty in relaxing one or two groups of muscles. Such individuals may have experienced excessive tension in these particular groups often as the consequences of prolonged, unremitting stress over many years. More time and effort must be spent in relaxing these particular groups. Given adequate attention and patience the signs of tension should gradually dissipate.

PROGRESSIVE MUSCLE RELAXATION EXERCISES

The method is called 'progressive' as it proceeds through all of the major muscle groups, contracting and relaxing them, one at a time, leading eventually to a completely relaxed state.

It may seem paradoxical at first to tense muscle groups if the purpose is to produce relaxation. The explanation is that all people, during their waking hours, have some level of tension (the adaptation level); the level varies from individual to individual. Research demonstrates that, when a group of muscles is tensed for a few seconds and then instantly relaxed, a greater decrease of tension may be achieved than by attempting to relax the muscles by 'letting go'; the momentum, as it were, allows the tension in the muscles to drop far below the adaptation level (Bernstein and Borkovec, 1973).

Progressive relaxation can be used to relax the body completely or to relax only certain parts. For example, an accountant whose work involves long hours each day at a desk may find that his neck and shoulder muscles become particularly tense. The progressive relaxation exercises could be utilized to ameliorate the tension.

BASIC TRAINING PROGRAMME

Sixteen muscle groups are progressively tensed and relaxed. Each group is tensed for approximately 7–8 seconds. After the tension has been released attention is focused on the relaxed group for some 15 seconds; the muscle group is tensed for a second time and relaxed in the manner described. Then the next muscle group is dealt with similarly. During the initial stages of training considerable care should be taken when tensing muscles in the neck, chest and legs; the training procedures should be discussed with your doctor if there is any indication of heart, respiratory or other serious problems. Before relaxation training remove your shoes.

The following instructions can be memorized by the reader or given by a friend. Alternatively, a tape recording of relaxation instructions, methods and exercises (basic, intermediate and advanced), may be obtained from the author, Dr L. E. Burns, Area Department of Clinical Psychology, Birch Hall Hospital, Rochdale OL12 9QN, Lancashire.

Relaxation of the arms

Sit back in your chair as comfortably as possible, breathe in and out normally, close your eyes and relax—relax completely.
Keep relaxed but clench your right fist.
Make the muscles of your lower arm and hand even tighter.
Monitor the feelings of tension.
Now relax; let all the tension go.
Allow the muscles of your lower arm and hand to become completely limp and loose.
Notice the contrast in the feelings.

Again clench your right fist—tighter and tighter.
Hold the tension and monitor the feelings.
Relax. There should be no signs of tension in your hand or lower arm.
Notice the feelings of relaxation again.

Keeping your right hand and lower arm as relaxed as possible, bring your right elbow into the back of the chair and press downwards,

contracting the bicep muscles (between your elbow and shoulder).
Press harder: make the muscles more tense.
Monitor the feelings of tightness.
Relax. Now let the tension dissipate immediately.
Observe the difference. Let the muscles relax further.

Now tense the right biceps again.
Make the muscles harder, tighter, more tense.
Monitor the feelings of tension.
Relax. Let the tension go completely.

Concentrate on the whole of your right arm. Relax it now, more and
  more deeply; relax it further and further.

(The exercises for the left hand, lower arm and biceps are exactly the
  same).

Relaxation of the facial muscles

Focus on your forehead muscles.
Raise your eyebrows upwards (keeping your eyes closed) and wrinkle
  your forehead.
Wrinkle it tighter. Hold it. Monitor the feelings.
Relax; smooth it out; let the tension go completely.
Now contract the forehead muscles—raise the eyebrows, frown,
  wrinkle the muscles.
Study the feelings of tension.
Relax; smooth the forehead muscles.
Observe the pleasant feelings of relaxation in the muscles.

Pay attention to your eyes, upper cheeks and nose.
Squint the eyes tightly; wrinkle the nose.
Hold it. Scrutinize the tension feelings.
Release the tension.

Examine the feelings of relaxation—allow the muscles to become
  even more deeply relaxed.
Once again, tense the eyes, upper cheeks and nose.
Now make the muscles considerably more tense.
Reflect on the feelings of tension.
Relax totally.

Now concentrate on your jaws and chin.
Clench your jaws; bite your teeth; pull the side of your mouth outwards.
Press your tongue hard against the roof of your mouth.
Look for the tension.
Relax. Appreciate the feelings of relaxation.
Now tense jaw, chin and tongue again—make the muscles more and more taut.
Release the tension; loosen the muscles completely.
Observe the feelings of relaxation.

Now focus on the whole of your face.
Allow all the muscles to become more and more deeply relaxed. No signs of tension; no signs of firmness.
Let the relaxation develop; let it grow deeper and deeper.

Relaxation of the neck muscles

Concentrate on the neck muscles.
Press your head firmly against the back of the chair.
Press back with more force, making the muscles more and more taut.
Monitor the feelings of tautness.
Relax. Let the tension dissipate completely.
Discriminate the feelings of relaxation from those of tension.
Repeat the exercise tensing the neck muscles.
Again, perceive the feelings of pressure.
Relax—let it go.
Monitor the enjoyable sensations of relaxation.

Relaxation of the shoulders, chest, lower back and stomach

Relax your whole body completely.
Take a slow deep breath.
While holding the breath, sit forward slightly, throw the chest out and bring the shoulder blades together, keeping the hands relaxed.
Hold a monitor the tension.
Relax. Exhale. Drop into the chair; let the tension go completely.

Notice the feelings of relaxation while breathing in and out normally.

Once again take a slow deep breath, sit forward, throw the chest out and bring the shoulder blades together.

Again observe the feelings of tightness.

Relax. Exhale. Let your body slump into the chair.

Breathe in and out normally.

Enjoy the relaxation feelings.

Concentrate on the stomach muscles.

Pull the muscles in, tightly.

Survey the feelings of tension.

Relax. Let the muscles become flaccid.

Scan the feelings of relaxation. Study them.

Draw the muscles of the stomach in.

Examine, once more, the feelings of tautness.

Now relax; let all signs of tension go.

Focus now on the whole of the main part of your body—shoulders, chest, stomach, back.

Let the whole of this area become more and more relaxed. Give in to the feelings of relaxation completely. Do not resist them. Allow yourself to become more and more deeply relaxed.

Relaxation of the thighs, calves and feet

Press your right heel into the floor. Press it down harder.

Notice the feelings of tension in the thigh.

Study that tension.

Relax. Keep relaxing. Monitor the relaxation.

Again, press your right heel into the floor.

Again, scrutinize the tense feelings.

Relax again. Let the tense feelings dissipate.

Reflect on the pleasant feelings of relaxation now.

Focus on the right calf.

Tense the muscles by curling the toes of your right foot downwards.

Make the muscles more tense.

Recognize the feelings of the rigid muscles.

Now let the feelings go. Just relax.
Again tighten up the calf muscles by curling the toes downwards.
Hold and observe the tense feelings.
Relax. Enjoy the feeling of comfort.

Concentrate on your right foot.
Tense it, by curling your toes upwards.
Have the muscles become more and more taut.
Monitor the feelings.
Relax. Let all the tension go out of the muscles.
Now flex your foot muscles again by curling your toes upwards.
Study the tension.
Let the tension go.
Notice how relaxed the foot muscles feel.

(The left thigh, calf and foot are relaxed in the same manner).

Increasing the relaxation response

Concentrate on your whole body—head, neck, shoulders, chest,
   stomach, lower back and legs.
Let your whole body sink into an even deeper state of relaxation.
Just give in to the feelings of relaxation. Do not resist them.
Allow your whole body to become more and more relaxed.
Continue to breathe in and out normally.
Concentrate now on your feet. Imagine that they are becoming
   heavy; heavy as a ton of lead.
Concentrate on your legs. Visualize that they are becoming more and
   more heavy; more and more relaxed.
Imagine the heaviness spreading into your stomach and chest
   regions; now into your neck and head.
Your hands and arms are becoming heavier, more and more relaxed.
Your whole body is becoming heavier and heavier.
Becoming so heavy now that its sinking into the chair . . . down . . .
   down . . . down, becoming more and more heavy, more and more
   relaxed.
Monitor the very pleasant feelings of deep relaxation; feelings of
   calmness and tranquillity.
Keep your thoughts on these feelings.
Just continue to relax.

Carry on relaxing for another 7–8 minutes. Use the basic training schedule daily for 7–10 days; then go on to the intermediate programme.

INTERMEDIATE TRAINING PROGRAMME

This programme is similar to the Basic Training Programme except that the sixteen muscle groups are combined to form seven groups. The seven groups are:

(1) Right hand and arm.
   The muscles of this group are contracted by clenching the fist while pressing the elbow into the back of the chair.
(2) Left hand and arm.
   Tensing method as in (1).
(3) Face.
   Squint eyes, clench jaws, push the teeth together, pull sides of mouth outwards.
(4) Neck.
   Press head firmly against back of chair.
(5) Main part of body.
   Take a slow deep breath; throw the chest out bringing the shoulder blades together while pulling in the muscles of the stomach.
(6) Right leg.
   Press the heel into the floor while curling the toes downwards.
(7) Left leg.
   Tensing method as in (6).

Then carry on the training session using the 'Increasing the Relaxation Response' section of the basic programme.

The intermediate training programme should be used daily for 7–10 days. Then commence the Advanced Programme.

ADVANCED TRAINING PROGRAMME

In this programme all of the seven groups of muscles referred to in the intermediate programme are combined to form one muscle group — i.e. the whole body.

The muscles are contracted on four occasions (remember that, as in the previous programmes, the muscles are tensed for 7–8 seconds and the relaxation period between the contractions should last for approximately 15 seconds). The procedure for the advanced training programme is as follows:

> Take a slow deep breath. Hold it.
> Sit forward slightly.
> Throw the chest out, pulling the stomach muscles in. Tense the facial muscles and press both heels into the floor, curling the toes downwards. Clench the fists and press the elbows into the back of the chair.
> Make all the muscles tighter and tighter.
> Monitor the feelings of tension all over the body.
> Relax by slumping into the chair and by exhaling. Let all the muscles throughout the body become totally limp.
> Breathe in and out normally.

After the muscles have been tensed on four occasions proceed with the 'Increasing the Relaxation Response' section of the basic programme.

Use the advanced training procedure on a daily basis for 7–10 days. After that period the programme may be used as appropriate. For example, on a daily basis to counteract chronic tension or two or three times a week to maintain the relaxation skills.

FACILITATING TRANSFER OF THE RELAXATION RESPONSE TO LIFE SITUATIONS

Although the individual can gain benefit from practising 20 minutes of relaxation daily, the ultimate goal is for him to use these skills to control tension in any area of his life. Just as an individual learns—over a period of time—to become tense, so the process can be reversed and the relaxation skills become habitual.

As mentioned previously, sometimes individuals become quite tense generally but may not be aware of it, apart from acute episodes when the state of arousal is very high. During the training sessions the use of differential monitoring of tension and relaxation should help to considerably increase the level of self-awareness. To facilitate the transfer of relaxation skills acquired during the training sessions the individual is asked to self-monitor his levels of tension, on a random basis, on several occasions during the course of a day. For example, tension may be monitored in the arms and neck while driving to work in the rush hour or while working at a desk. Having assessed the state, general or differential relaxation skills may be brought into play. The aim is for internal cues of tension to automatically trigger a relaxation response. Clearly there are many environmental events which can evoke stressful reactions. Having identified such potentially stressful events the goal should be to routinely relax in their presence; for example, at meetings, interviews, et cetera. In time such events can become strongly associated with the relaxation response.

Chapter 5
Removing Surplus Anxiety

TO BEGIN WITH

Worry has important survival values: without it life would be pretty short and, no doubt, even more unpleasant. Worry helps us to anticipate the hazards of life, to devise means of coping with problems and to examine, in imagination, the kinds of solutions that may be helpful. Constructive worry could take the form of envisaging a difficult interview in which certain awkward questions are posed to which we must find the effective answers; or rehearsing the excuses one might offer for arriving late at an important business meeting; or the ways in which one might deal with losing one's thread in the middle of a public speech. There are obviously many occasions when each of us entertains such thoughts, since life provides ample opportunity for worry.

Of course, worry in the sense of imagining some future event of concern, and the deliberate rehearsal of problem-solving strategies can be useful and is not really very different from any other problem-solving activity except in that it is accompanied by an unpleasant feeling state. There are two other characteristics of constructive worry that deserve mention. First, once the solution to the problem has been arrived at, or once the real problem has been met, we are then free from preoccupations of this kind. Second, the worry clearly has to do with some real cause for concern and the population at large would be likely to agree that it is reasonable to experience that concern.

Unconstructive or pathological worry is quite different in obvious ways. Often the object of concern is trivial or so statistically remote that the public generally would not think it a reasonable cause. Furthermore, the degree of negative feeling (depression, anxiety) is often rather greater than in the case of constructive worrying. Nor is it problem-solving in character, but rather tends to take the form of a repetitive re-statement of the problem instead of examining possibly helpful solutions. Finally, the worry tends to be persistent and

56

nags at the individual before, during and even after the event.

Of course, such worries are within the realm of everyone's experience, but one would hope to reduce the frequency with which they occur and restrict their impact on one's life. We hope not to become chronic worriers, with a mental apparatus tuned to respond in a wholly exaggerated way to every stimulus, however ephemeral. A recent example of chronic worrying had seized upon the latest ripple on the surface of his life by grossly over-reacting to the news that his daughter wished, for the first time, to go to a disco! After long and harrowing discussion with her he finally agreed to allow her to go, not to pick her up there in his car, and to go to bed rather than wait. In turn, she had promised that there would be absolutely 'no nonsense' and that she would come straight home with her friend and would arrive promptly at 11.15 p.m. Her father dutifully went to bed on the night in question but, of course, had every intention of staying awake until his daughter's return and so kept his eye on the bedside clock. He noticed a familiar feeling of mounting anxiety as the hands of the clock approached the agreed time of her return and, when no key was heard in the door by 11.15, his unconstructive worries began in earnest. Between 11.15 and 11.30 (when she actually arrived home) he 'created' a series of horrifying fantasies in which his daughter played a leading role as the victim of a hit-and-run driver, the object of an assault by a sex-crazed psychopath, and so on. By the time she arrived home he had become so overwrought that he was seized by the impulse to leap out of bed and belabour her for putting him through such mental agony. As he put it to me 'well, you do worry, don't you doctor?'.

Of course one does, but not in this way or on such minimal provocation and with such intensity! One also notes that the heightened emotion has spilled over and is directed towards the daughter whose guilt is pretty marginal in this case — certainly not justifying the feelings of outrage inspired in her father.

The temptation may arise to reject any personal implication in the above example — surely one does not oneself behave in this unbalanced manner! Yet, while the specific example may not be true of an individual, examples of such exaggerated reactions are not uncommon where the unconstructive worry and anxiety have become sufficiently intense or prolonged to debilitate, impair our efficiency, and cause numerous other secondary problems.

Indeed, making a list of one's worries, rating their intensity, frequency and 'genuineness' is a good way of beginning to assume some control over them. A few common preoccupations, to help you in compiling your personal list, are shown in Table 4.

Table 4   Rating of common preoccupatons

	Frequency	Intensity	Likelihood of happening
	0 1 2	0 1 2	0 1 2
Fear of losing your job			
Fear of losing sexual potency			
Fear of dying			
Fear of heights			
Fear of strangers			
Fear of being made to look foolish			
Fear of flying or travel			
Fear of losing control			
Worry about possible ill-health			
Worry about criticism by others			
Worry about dependents, et cetera			

0 = Not at all; 1 = moderate; 2 = high.

HOW SUPERFLUOUS ANXIETY DEVELOPS

Most of us would subscribe to the notion that a little anxiety is a good thing, by which we mean that anxiety, in moderation, can act as a spur or motivating force. It is, perhaps, an essential element in preparing for a race, an examination or some other occasion where success and achievement matter.

In fact we can argue that this kind of 'push' must have had survival value since, in its milder forms, anxiety is not an entirely unpleasant state. There is really no need to labour this point, since the pleasure of 'nerve-tingling excitement' is common to our experience.

The problem with anxiety, unfortunately, is that it appears to readily assume proportions that are entirely unhelpful, and that it has a tendency to become attached to quite innocuous activities and situations.

To take the first of these points, a great deal of experimental work has been gathered to show that high levels of anxiety interfere with task performance and result in lowered efficiency and the relationship between anxiety and performance conforms to an inverted 'U' shape

(Figure 1). As can be seen, a modest increase in anxiety is depicted as improving performance but, thereafter, increasing levels of anxiety produce marked deterioration.

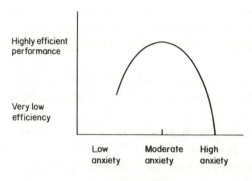

Highly efficient performance

Very low efficiency

Low anxiety | Moderate anxiety | High anxiety

Figure 1

Obviously, for reasons of performance efficiency alone we would want to limit the amount of anxiety experienced but, of course, we would also wish to avoid the unpleasant nature of the feelings associated with high anxiety, as well as the remorse and embarrassment which might be occasioned by abysmal performance.

The second point is equally important. Clearly survival has depended upon man's capacity to learn quickly and well, particularly where dangerous situations are involved, so that 'the burned child dreads the fire'. Indeed, it is just as well that one incident of its kind is sufficient to protect the organism from committing the same mistake again, but sometimes the super-efficiency with which learning takes place means not only that the fear or anxiety generated is greatly exaggerated, but that the fear reaction has spread to a number of quite innocuous but related circumstances.

For example, in the case of the burned child, an accident of this kind may provoke such an intense and enduring fear that the child can no longer make sensible use of the fire when he is cold, his aversion outweighing his need to keep warm. Further, we may find that the child not only fears the glowing coals, but also things associated with them — the brass poker, and tongs, the ornaments on the mantelshelf, and the blue and white tiles which form part of the fireplace. Such is the nature of aversive learning that there can be this generalization or *spread* of fear to objects or circumstances which have not themselves been directly experienced as harmful.

At this point, the reactions of those who consider themselves to be 'well-adjusted' and free from unwanted anxiety might well be sympathetic but dismissive — the burned child situation simply does not apply to them. Yet a detailed self-appraisal, in the most objective way one can manage, can almost certainly show otherwise. In fact the evidence suggests that, effectively, no-one manages to get through life without experiencing some degree of unwanted and *unnecessary* anxiety.

How many of us with teenage children lie awake waiting for them to arrive home safely, worrying as to their whereabouts and, perhaps, allowing unpleasant and frightening ideas to invade our minds? How many will recognize the fruitlessness of such worry, since it is not problem-solving, achieves nothing constructive, and deprives us of much-needed sleep. Further, such worry and tension may lead the sufferer to discharge the anxiety in the form of verbal abuse of the offending teenager, creating new and very real problems in relationships. How many of us worry needlessly about what others will think of us on account of some really rather trivial occurrence? How many are excessively anxious about the security of what may well be a safe job, or the possibility of serious illness if we are 40 and have a headache? How many false coronary heart attacks, brain tumours, stomach cancers and so on, are there in each day? Many thousands, one suspects, and certainly many times the number of those who actually have cause to worry about such matters.

Mr K., an executive in a large retail group, had been working under considerable pressure for a few months. The business recession had made serious inroads into profits and this had led Mr K. to redouble his efforts for the company. Indeed, he spent so much time away from home trying to improve sales figures that his relationship with his family suffered and, understandably, he felt that everything he had worked for and cared about was threatened. At the height of his misery a new thunderbolt struck — while shaving one morning he felt a sharp pain in his chest. Believing this to be a heart attack he consulted his GP and a heart specialist, both of whom were able to reassure him that there was nothing physically wrong.

He felt happier about the matter but, a few days later, the pain returned during a business lunch and, seeing Mr K.'s anxiety and pallor, his colleagues called an ambulance. The hospital to which he was taken were able to reassure Mr K. that there was no heart attack and no other sign of physical abnormality and he returned to work next day.

However, such incidents were repeated on several more occasions and Mr K. became quite convinced that he had had a number of heart attacks, none of which had been properly diagnosed. Only reluctantly did he come to accept that his problems were the reaction to the self-imposed stresses of his job.

Fortunately, few of us are so obviously affected by stress, but unwanted anxieties occur in all of us and affect our lives in ways that we rarely clarify in a systematic and organized manner. Some of these anxieties may never surface in a public way, but remain as highly personal and secret sources of tension that generate a sense of shame and concern that anyone else might come to know of them (although their indirect manifestations are very frequently detectable by others). Yet those anxieties and tensions attaching to our domestic lives that have been difficult to resolve serve to influence our working lives and the problems deriving from our working situations can spill over into domestic existence to mar our family relationships. Such problems are the subject of musical-hall jokes but to the sufferer there is real pain and a desire to escape from the bondage of fear, anxiety and worry and, often, the signs of distress emerge in apparently inappropriate forms.

In one such case a company accountant in his 30s noticed, at first, a slight and then a rapidly growing apprehension concerning public presentations of financial data. He was well aware of the ludicrously inappropriate anxiety since all was well with both the company and his own figures, but the fear grew until it eventually prevented him from carrying out any part of his work involving an audience. Certainly, in this case, a severe reaction but not uncommon in its focus since the fear of *being found at fault in a public setting* is widespread.

A similar reaction was found in a young executive who found it quite impossible to eat in the presence of strangers although, as an intelligent and generally well-balanced individual, he could recognize the absurdity of his anxiety. Nevertheless, the thought (and feeling) that he might vomit in public, with all the humiliating consequences this would carry, were irresistible and he contrived patently flimsy reasons for avoiding eating with anyone but his own family. Clearly, his working life was very much hampered by the problem.

Intense anxiety also characterized a company director in situations which involved interactions with people of assertive and abrasive temperament. He was well aware that dealing with such individuals was part of his job and that the physical risks to himself in doing so were really non-existent. Yet he found it intensely upsetting to face an interview or meeting with an individual showing even a trace of belligerence and his avoidance strategies became obvious to his colleagues.

In yet another example, a property developer could not rid himself of anxieties about his work even though he could recognize that these involved (comparatively) trivial matters and constituted no serious threat to himself or his company. Nevertheless, the mistake made, or that which he could possibly make in the next 'deal' to be concluded, nagged at him constantly and destroyed his peace of mind.

There are, of course, many such examples all bearing the hallmarks of unreasonableness, intensity, persistence and often the clear recognition by the person involved that the worry is unnecessary and foolish. One of the behavioural strategies for dealing with such problems is known as systematic desensitization; it is particularly useful where there is some strong single source of anxiety.

Systematic desensitization

Most of us recognize that irrational or unreasonable fears are not always overcome by facing up to and confronting the difficulty head-on, so to speak. There are good reasons why one should avoid running away from problems and there is no doubt that the advice given to the pilot who crashes—take up another machine at once—is very sound. Once one has *reduced anxiety by walking away from the situation* it becomes extremely difficult to go back again. But the validity of not-running-away does nothing to erode the general rule that fear is most effectively eliminated on a little-by-little basis.

Take, for example, the common anxieties of childhood, such as fear of the dark, of dogs, of school, and so on, where a gradual approach is both easy and demonstrably beneficial. The idea is essentially simple and one that many parents have employed simply because it makes good sense and works empirically, rather than from a knowledge of sophisticated psychological principles.

As applied to fear of the dark, it is important to think of the range of situations that represents points along a continuum from the most to the least feared (from complete darkness, perhaps,* to full illumination). Usually it is found that a fully-lighted bedroom is not at all

---

* The qualification is necessary here since complete darkness may not be quite as frightening as the glimmer of light which allows 'threatening' shadows to appear.

alarming but, as the amount of light is progressively decreased, so the fear grows in magnitude. 'Dimmer' switches are the most convenient way to alter the amount of light available and, if available, all the 'stages' needed can be readily arranged. It is important to take care that the child is given time to get used to each stage (i.e. to experience the *absence of apprehension*) before going on to the next one if we are to make effective use of the little-by-little approach.

The approach accords with common sense and is a good example of how psychological principles agree with what we *know* to be true. But psychology often adds a little to what is obvious and it is important not to lose sight of this since effectiveness is greatly enhanced when we introduce a degree of sophistication. Indeed, this additional expertise can make all the difference to the outcome and it is the purpose of this chapter to illuminate the refinements which transform sensible advice into the successful application of scientific principle.

It is convenient to divide the substance of what is to be said into three separate sections: getting the problem right, setting the stage for self-treatment, and the practical business of applying the therapy.

Posing the problem

Often this has the appearance of being a simple matter, but there are decided advantages to taking the examination of the problem more seriously. It is not enough, for example, to conclude that the problem is 'worrying about looking foolish in public', or 'worrying about the managing director's attitude to oneself', since no course of action (at least, not one that is useful) follows from such statements. What is needed is an analysis of the nature of the anxiety which, perhaps, is easiest to understand with reference to the comparatively simple problem of spider phobia.

Here, one can see, the fear is not of some vague and hypothetical spider but rather of *specific characteristics* that one has come to dread. For example, we may find that a dead spider is not as worrying as a living specimen; a black one is far more frightening than one which is light coloured; a large spider evokes more problems than one which is small, and so on. Perhaps the distance separating us from the spider, the fact that it is trapped in a jam jar, the hairiness of appearance and numerous other characteristics will all help to define the problem in the *manageable operational* terms we need. One can readily see, then, how such descriptions might allow us to arrange the anxiety stimulus (spiders) along a continuum from 'most' to 'least' feared in an orderly way—an essential if we are to implement the little-by-little approach.

A fear of flying is surprisingly common. Often this is not crippling in nature, but sufficiently discomforting to need attention and, certainly, an experience one might prefer to be without. It is not, of course, simply the adverse feeling during the flight itself that prompts the desire for change, but the anticipatory anxiety, the avoidance-of-flying stratagems, the prevarication and the awareness that others are becoming aware of the problem, all of which add to the feelings of discomfort and distress.

Clearly the mere notion of 'flying' is an inadequate basis for fear and, more pertinently, does not enable one to get to grips with the anxiety produced nor with its treatment. Rather, when we analyse the problem it is apparent that the fear is a response to the presence of certain stimuli or situations, such as checking in one's bags at the airport, waiting in the departure lounge, boarding the plane, hearing the aircraft door finally closing, hurtling down the runway, rising into the air, and so on. Looked at in this way it becomes clear that the anxiety about flying can be broken down into components, each of which may be the stimulus to a greater or lesser degree of discomfort, so that 'waiting-in-the-departure-lounge-and-sipping-a-cup-of-coffee' is less difficult to deal with than 'turbulence-experienced-on-entering-cloud-formations'.

Other areas of difficulty may not always lend themselves to such obviously simple analysis, and careful thought is needed to arrive at useful conclusions. The case of the Company Director referred to earlier, for example, requires a consideration of what it is that inspires anxiety—appearance, manner, abruptness, power wielded, verbal skills, and so on. We will need to know how these characteristics were revealed in the real-life situation and the meaningful thread that runs through them.

In fact the problem is more apparent than real since the identification of a meaningful theme or thread arises out of the identification of the elements that occasion fear. It is important, however, to recognize the full range of situations that inspire similar anxiety, so that the elements that produce fear can be adequately manipulated. For example, it is not simply the assertive individual's rasping voice which produces the adverse effect, but a similar voice when employed by others, albeit to lesser effect. It is not just the pointed question posed by one particular individual that triggers anxiety, but to some degree a question posed in a similar way by anyone. In short, the analysis of the *elements* which occasion the anxiety reaction enables one to see clearly how the theme is made up and allows one to arrange these elements in accordance with the little-by-little rule.

Setting the scene for self-treatment

There are two main tasks to accomplish once the problem has been determined. First, the items or elements which define the problem must be arranged in their proper order and appropriate combinations so that anxiety can be elicited in a greater or lesser degree. This is the construction of the 'hierarchy'. Secondly, it is necessary to prepare a means of *counteracting* any anxiety experienced so that the elements progressively lose their capacity to evoke such a reaction. In effect the procedure involves:

(a) Exposing oneself progressively to situations that represent increasing amounts of anxiety.
(b) Counteracting any anxiety experienced, even though it may be experienced in only small amounts.

At face value, both tasks seem to involve considerable difficulties. How is it possible, one may ask, to so arrange one's life that the sources of anxiety within it occur in a neat and systematic way? How is it possible, also, to prevent the experience of anxiety and, indeed, is not the inability to do so the very essence of the problem?

Both difficulties, fortunately, are reasonably easy to overcome.

How to present anxiety elements

It is commonly believed that the world outside ourselves is quite different from the 'inner world' of one's mind. In some obvious ways this is indeed so, but it is apparent that these two 'worlds' merge and blend together—'Indeed, the appreciation and knowledge of the world outside *can* only be through one's own mental processes. But the crucial point to make here is that, for practical therapeutic purposes, what happens *in the mind* can be regarded as essentially equivalent to what is happening in the 'real' world. In short, we can make use of fantasy and imagination to create an inner world which effectively parallels the external one.

This is obviously a tremendous help in dealing with the reservation stated earlier. We cannot manage to make the *external* world conform to the carefully arranged hierarchy of anxiety situations, but it is entirely possible to achieve this *in imagination*. We can, if we wish, dwell only upon certain elements in a feared situation, or we may 'fix' a situation which, in the real world, would stubbornly refuse to remain static. For example, I am able to imagine a small kitten, sitting quietly in front of an open fire, wearing a blue ribbon from which hangs a small silver bell, and so on. In the 'real' world, the kitten would perhaps fail to remain just as I depicted it; maybe it would roll over, stretch, walk towards me, or whatever; but in my imagination I can fix this scene precisely.

So, all we need to do is to present to ourselves the elements from the problem situations *imaginally*. Not only will this simplify matters very considerably (imagining boarding a plane being very much easier and quicker to arrange than doing so in the real world!), but the effect on our reactions will be *much the same* as if the same event were to occur in the real world.*

This is not easy to accept at first but, as a matter of well-documented fact, it turns out to be the case. Indeed, it has been repeatedly demonstrated that once we have become accustomed to the anxiety-evoking elements *in imagination* we will have acquired a greater capacity for dealing with the same elements as they occur in the external world. Having said this, however, it is important to add the qualification that there are certain rules to be observed if we want to achieve the desired affect. These are:

(1)   The elements should be encapsulated in a short 'scene' which we deliberately create in imagination.
(2)   The scene should last for only a short time, say 10–20 seconds.
(3)   It is terminated *at once* if any sense of discomfort (anxiety) is experienced.
(4)   If no 'twinge' of anxiety occurs in the 19–20 seconds exposure then the scene is switched to the relaxation scene (to be described later) before being presented again.
(5)   The same scene is presented repeatedly until no anxiety is experienced, say, for three successive presentations.
(6)   When the criterion (under (5), above) is reached, the whole process is repeated, this time using the next step in the hierarchy.

---

* You may, of course, include a situation which you have never personally experienced. What counts is that such a situation *would*, if it were encountered, cause discomfort.

(7)   The scenes should be realistic and vivid.

The process is in fact very simple. Brief scenes involving anxiety elements are imagined in a systematic and controlled way and in this manner a tolerance for the most anxiety-evoking situations is built-up.

Counteracting anxiety produced

In the routine described above, it may be that only the faintest unease is detectable, or perhaps an entire absence of discomfort, when the scenes are imagined. This is not unusual and certainly facilitates the speed with which progress will be made.* More often a small amount of anxiety is felt; in this case it should prompt the abrupt termination of the scene as described in (3) above. After a short period of relaxation the scene causing the anxious reaction should be presented again, and this sequence is repeated until the reaction no longer occurs. To some extent this is achieved by the sheer repetition of the scene, but an important aid is the muscle relaxation which has been described in an earlier chapter. In fact the whole treatment process described here is conducted under conditions of relaxation in order to facilitate the opportunity to learn to associate the elements employed with a calm feeling state, rather than one characterized by tension and anxiety.

Whenever the anxiety scene is terminated, for whatever reason, it has been found helpful to then imagine a particular scene associated with relaxation, for example relating to especially pleasant recollections of a holiday. Such a scene might involve lying on a pleasant beach under a warm sun with the clear cool water of the sea just a few feet away . . ., et cetera. In other words, during the presentation of the 'anxiety' scenes to oneself an effort is made to control and eliminate even the smallest traces of discomfort by relaxing physically, but should some degree of discomfort be experienced, then the anxiety scene is 'switched off' and *immediately replaced* by the pleasant scene, as described, and a return to a very relaxed muscle condition.

We can now consider how the complete programme of inquiry and treatment is assembled and then give examples of some hierarchies of anxiety which might help to clarify the procedure.

---

*It should be said that a lack of concern may be experienced as a result of not depicting the scene adequately. This is undesirable and will not produce effective results.

STEPS IN SELF—TREATMENT OF ANXIETY

(1) First diagnose the problem. The analysis is achieved by identifying the elements involved and putting these into a logical order and combinations.

(2) Build a hierarchy of such elements and try to quantify the reactions these would produce from 100 (most anxious) to 5 (minimally upset). Try to arrange combinations of elements which represent each of 20 points on a scale of subjective disturbance, e.g. 5, 10, 15, 20, up to 100.

(3) Each point should involve a simple scene which one can imagine easily and with clarity.

(4) Before presenting the scenes in a treatment context, learn to relax (as described in Chapter 4) and select a relaxation scene which has pleasant connotations.

(5) Choose a time when you can be undisturbed for about 40 minutes or so and relax as well as you can in a comfortable chair. Allow your mind to dwell upon the relaxation scene.

(6) When you are quite calm and completely at ease, turn your attention to the matter represented by the first step in your hierarchy. 'See' the scene as clearly and realistically as possible for about 15–20 seconds and then go back to the relaxation scene again, as in (5) above.

(7) If you should experience some discomfort as a reaction to the 'anxiety' scene depicted, turn your mind away from it at once and go back to your relaxation scene; ensure that you are fully relaxed before repeating the same scene again.

(8) Continue presenting each scene until, on three successive occasions, no anxiety or discomfort is experienced.

(9) After achieving the criterion set out in (8) above, move to the next step in your 'hierarchy' of scenes and repeat the same process set out in (6)–(8).

(10) Continue dealing with each step in the same way until you have eliminated any trace of anxiety to every point in your hierarchy.

In general

Obviously, in such a brief presentation of the technique, not everything can be said. However, you can have confidence in the effectiveness of a graduated approach as a valuable help to overcoming unwanted anxiety. Take time and trouble in analysing the nature of your aversive reactions and exercise care in building the hierarchy to deal with it. Remember that what you are doing not only makes sense but actually works. What you are doing in observing the rules given here is to refine, in the light of scientific research, what common sense dictates.

Just how the technique works in theoretical terms is still a matter of dispute. To some extent, perhaps, mere exposure to a small amount of anxiety-making stimuli may be helpful; or it could be that an essential ingredient is the active inhibition of that anxiety, e.g. by relaxation. It may be that the technique simply affords practice in developing the capacity to shift the focus of attention from anxiety-evoking topics to those which are neutral or pleasant in character. Whatever the mechanisms, the results obtained are often excellent and the amount of work needed to achieve benefit is amply repaid.

Do not allow the simplicity of the technique to affect the energy and enthusiasm you bring to bear in your personal training; the exercises must be carried out rigorously and systematically if you are to profit fully from them and, in this sense, there is a parallel between physical and psychological fitness.

Finally, the use of these strategies does not imply that you are a confirmed neurotic. Most people have developed some kind of 'phobic' reaction at one time or other, but perhaps do little about it if it is an infrequent nuisance or a minor irritation. Use the technique to deal with minor amounts of superfluous emotional reactions that you would wish to lose and which impair your personal effectiveness.

Below are examples of hierarchies which deal with particular anxiety themes. They are only illustrative and may not represent the ordering of 'scenes' or items as you would arrange them. Nevertheless, they show the kind of thing which is needed and will help you in planning your own hierarchy.

A hierarchy for anxiety about public speaking

	Degree of anxiety or disturbance caused	
(1)	100	Presenting a serious managerial problem to an unsympathetic meeting of the company board —interruptions frequently made.
(2)	95	Presenting as above, but to a more understanding audience.

(3)	90	As in (1) but to a small, special committee, instead of the full board.
(4)	85	Giving a talk to a large gathering of the Rotary Club at a local hall.
(5)	80	Being interviewed live for a TV news item.
(6)	75	Receiving a telephone call from the Managing Director to attend a special Board Meeting as in (2) above.
(7)	70	Briefly introducing a speaker to a large audience at a Women's Institute meeting.
(8)	65	Driving to the meeting as in (1) above.
(9)	60	Receiving a letter requesting attendance next week at a meeting as in (3) above.
(10)	55	Making a brief, recorded, TV appearance.
(11)	50	Giving a speech at Prize Giving at your old school.
(12)	45	Standing up and heckling a speaker in a crowded hall at a political meeting.
(13)	40	Making a prepared statement to a small workforce delegation about altered conditions of employment.
(14)	35	Receiving a telephone call and invitation from the headmaster with reference to (11) above.
(15)	30	Giving a 'pep' talk to the members of your department at work.
(16)	25	Acting as chairman in a light-hearted debate at the works social club.
(17)	20	'Officiating' for an hour at the Youth Club disco patronized by your daughter.
(18)	15	Giving directions to a group of tourists you meet in an art gallery.
(19)	10	Being telephoned by the producer in respect of (10) above.
(20)	5	Telling six of your colleagues in the staff dining room about some news item you have read.

A hierarchy for fear of flying

| (1) | 100 | The captain announces a delay in take-off due to a mechanical problem. |

(2)	95	The aircraft has just lifted off the runway at the start of its journey.
(3)	90	The plane runs into turbulence and you are requested to fasten your seatbelt.
(4)	85	The captain announces that a delay in landing is expected.
(5)	80	The aircraft makes an unexpected descent which 'leaves your stomach behind'.
(6)	75	The aircraft begins its descent through thick cloud.
(7)	70	The captain announces that there are poor weather conditions at your destination.
(8)	65	The plane begins its take-off along the runway, the engines making a tremendous noise.
(9)	60	The plane taxies out towards the runway, the tyres 'thumping' over the cracks in the tarmac.
(10)	55	Sitting in the crowded cabin, the door closed, waiting for the plane to begin to move off.
(11)	50	Fastening your seatbelt and seeing the cabin door being finally closed by the stewardess.
(12)	45	Half-way up the steps leading into the body of the aircraft.
(13)	40	Walking across the tarmac towards the steps leading into the plane.
(14)	35	Waiting at the 'gate' before walking across to the plane.
(15)	30	Walking along a long corridor towards the 'gate'.
(16)	25	Waiting in the departure lounge half an hour before your flight is to be called.
(17)	20	Checking-in your case at the airport.
(18)	15	Being driven to the airport.
(19)	10	Having breakfast on the morning that you are to catch your flight.
(20)	5	Receiving your flight tickets in the mail.

Chapter 6
Cognitive Methods in the Management of Stress

In the first chapter reference was made to the fact that cognitive distortions can arise in response to stressful events. Consider the following situation. Two executives, on separate occasions, present papers at important conferences. Both have essentially the same speaking skills but they differ in their level of speech-anxiety. One executive has high speech-anxiety; the other low. Some members of the audience leave their seats and walk out of the hall during each presentation. What do the speakers say about the exodus? The executive with the high speech-anxiety might self-verbalize: 'My God, they are leaving the hall. My presentation must be dreadful and be lacking in interest. I knew I was a bad speaker'. These self-statements are a manifestation of anxiety; in themselves they evoke further anxiety, perhaps panic, and, in turn, become self-fulfilling prophecies. On the other hand, the executive with low speech-anxiety is more likely to attribute their leaving to external events such as the nearness of lunch or other considerations. His self-verbalization is more likely to be along the lines, 'It's getting near lunch time and I guess they wish to have a drink before eating. What a pity; they are going to miss a good presentation.'

Thus, the executive with high-level anxiety may engage in self-defeating, self-deprecating, anxiety-generating and often irrational patterns of thinking. These evaluative patterns are frequently ruminative in nature and highly unproductive; they can lead to a loss of self-esteem, demoralization and mood states such as depression and anger. This executive tends to be self-oriented and to personalize the challenges with which he is confronted.

A number of types of cognitive distortion may arise; these may lead to, and help maintain, an individual's belief in the validity of his negative concepts. Seven types of cognitive distortion may be identified.

72

(1) Overgeneralization.

Here the individual draws some general rule or conclusion as a result of one or a few isolated episodes; this conclusion is then applied across the board to similar or dissimilar circumstances.

(2) Selective abstraction.

This error in thinking involves concentrating on some detail taken out of context while concurrently ignoring more conspicuous features of the event; the experience is conceptualized on the basis of this detail.

(3) Arbitrary inference.

The individual makes a specific inference in the absence of evidence to support the conclusion; indeed, the evidence may even be to the contrary.

(4) Magnification.

This type of distortion can be seen when the individual grossly magnifies and gives excessive prominence to the importance of an event.

(5) Minimization.

Here the individual distorts the significance by grossly playing down the import of the event.

(6) Dichotomous thinking.

All experiences are placed in one of two categories: impeccable or defective, brilliant or crass. Usually the individual classifies himself in the most negative way.

(7) Personalization.

This type of cognitive distortion refers to the individual's proclivity to associate various external events, especially negative ones, to himself when there is no rational basis for making the judgement.

Unfortunately, the individual may take these kinds of irrational cognitions seriously; he may place a high degree of certainty in his thoughts and, as a consequence, tends to experience many aversive emotions; he then takes these emotional experiences as confirmatory evidence that his cognitions are, in fact, true. Thus there is a pattern of circular reasoning. The individual frequently fails to appreciate that his aversive emotional reaction is evoked and maintained by his internal dialogue. Irrational cognitions concerning incompetence, for example, can lead to feelings of worthlessness and depression which, in turn, lead to avoidance of business associates and friends. The change in his behaviour and the consequences of this in terms of impaired relationships reinforce the irrational cognitions.

Frequently there may be a loss of libido, an impaired appetite, sleep disturbance and a preoccupation with bodily symptoms; the individual is trapped into a self-perpetuating system which is closed. The irrational, self-defeating cognitions, the aversive emotional states, the maladaptive behaviour and the bodily symptoms continue to interact with, and reinforce, each other. This cycle may evolve insidiously over a period of time and may be accompanied by an increase in alcohol consumption or a need for tranquillizers. Clearly, in order to break this cycle, it is necessary to have the individual evaluate his internal dialogue in a rational manner and to give him insight into the fact that cognitive distortions may directly arise from misinterpretations of external or internal events. It is perhaps surprising that some executives and managers who are capable of making appropriate high-level decisions based on objectivity seem unable to apply a similar process when evaluating aspects of their own performance; this evaluation, as we have seen, may be distorted, hypercritical and unreasonably stringent.

Recognizing that cognitive distortions can have such a profound effect on emotions and behaviour, how can the individual help himself to modity his irrational cognitions? One approach of potential value is Rational Emotive Therapy (RET) which was first presented by Albert Ellis in 1955. Like the behavioural approach, RET assumes that virtually everything the individual does includes important learning elements.

Central to RET theory are the views of Epictetus some 2000 years ago: 'Men are disturbed not by things but by the views they take of them'.

The theory of RET can be put within the ABCDE framework.

At point A (some Activating Experience/Event) something transpires. For example, an executive has a good job and is made redundant.

At point C, the Consequence (emotional or behavioural), the executive responds to the situation at A and feels depressed and angry about the job loss, which may result in apathy and withdrawal.

As the behavioural and emotional consequence (C) almost immediately and directly succeeds the episode of the Activating Event (A), the individual tends to assume that A is the cause of C with the result that an irrational conclusion may be drawn such as 'I have lost an excellent position and, as a consequence of that loss, I am depressed, angry and apathetic.'

According to RET theory this conclusion represents a *non sequitur*. The emotional reaction stems from B, the Belief about A: 'I was happy with the position I had; it offered good prospects. As I did not wish to lose the position, I believe the loss to be terrible and disadvantageous.' Consider a different Belief about A: if the executive had felt indifferent or unconcerned about the job: 'It's not of major importance whether I keep the job or not', he would experience the consequence at C of indifference.

Thus, if the executive, at point B, merely desires the job and says 'It would be preferable if I had this job but, if I am made redundant, well, too bad!; it would be unfortunate but it's hardly the end of the world', then he will feel only disappointment or regret on the loss of the job. However, if he believes desperately that this job is of dire necessity and that he *must* have it, and that it would be the most major catastrophe if he were made redundant, then he may well experience depression, anger and near total inadequacy at point C which may lead to demoralization and an inability to compete effectively in the job market. The executive, then, is mainly responsible for his own consequences at C by emotively believing certain things at B—the individual's largely learned or acquired Belief System.

Of course, in reality, there may be virtually no chance of the executive losing his job but he might wrongly *think* that he will lose it and engage in ruminative, irrational thinking about the minuscule possibility of losing it; with these Beliefs he could effortlessly become depressed and demoralized.

Once an individual accepts that there is a very close relationship between what he things and the way he feels, he can appreciably make his emotions subject to his will. His ability to detect beliefs based on irrational considerations is important in this process.

According to Albert Ellis, many irrational beliefs include in them the word 'must' or 'should' although some of the beliefs merely consist of unrealistic and unempirical statements. The redundant executive may be unsuccessful, despite efforts, in obtaining an appropriate position and he might make the following statement: 'I am not going to get a suitable job again. That's the end of my career'. This conclusion would be irrational as it is made from a limited database: a rational conclusion he can make is that the data merely inform him that it is going to take time to obtain an appropriate position; in the meantime he can anticipate further possible rejections and consequent frustration. But to conclude that he will never find suitable employment again or that it is the end of his career represents an overgeneralization from the available data, and distorts reality.

Of course it is possible that these irrational conclusions may have some degree of validity, but probably very little. Ellis defines irrationality as any thought, emotional state or behaviour which leads to self-defeating or self-destructive consequences which significantly interfere with the adaptive functioning of the individual. Irrationality has several important components: as we have seen previously, the individual believes that irrationality accords with reality when in some significant aspect it does not do so. Individuals with irrational beliefs appear to deprecate or refuse to accept themselves; the irrationality interferes with interpersonal relationships and social activity; it impedes job satisfaction and obstructs their own best interests in other respects.

Ellis argues that irrationalities can be seen in humans from all social and cultural backgrounds; thus, people hold strong prejudices, resort to different kinds of illogical thinking, acquire and maintain self-defeating habits, et cetera. This is true of highly intelligent, well-educated and relatively undisturbed people; although they may hold fewer irrationalities or show more flexibility in their thinking, they still engage in magical-type thinking. If some so-called 'expert' holds very strong views about some matter, it must have objective reality, as if he has a monopoly on rational behaviour!

Insight into one's irrational behaviour is a step forward to modifying it but may not, in itself, be sufficient to bring about lasting change. Thus, the harmful effects of smoking may be recognized but the individual engages in the behaviour just the same. It seems as if some individuals often find it easier to learn self-defeating rather than non-self-defeating behaviour; perhaps they overlearn their defeating behaviours at an early age or perhaps the various irrationalities have some kind of biological roots or predisposition so that the early conditionability itself is a significant part of innate fallibility, as Ellis believes.

What then can the individual do to help overcome irrational beliefs and the aversive emotional consequences? This consideration brings us to point D in the RET paradigm: Disputing, Debating, Discriminating and Defining. RET uses the logico-empirical of scientific questioning and challenging. During the process the individual asks himself the questions: What is the evidence for my conclusion? Are there other explanations? Can I define it in ways in which it has truth or falseness? These rhetorical questions are designed to dispute and modify the irrational beliefs. RET disputing involves several types of cognitive restructuring:

(1) Detecting the irrationalities.
(2) Debating against the irrationalities.
(3) Discriminating between rational and irrational thinking.
(4) Defining so as to prevent overgeneralizing or other types of cognitive distortion and to maintain closer contact with reality.

Point E refers to the individual acquiring a new Effect or philosophy which helps him to think more rationally and constructively about himself and the world in which he lives; he begins to incorporate semi-automatically the disputing techniques at point D. Thus, in the example given concerning the redundant executive who believes that he will not obtain suitable employment and that his career is at an end, and who may be depressed and apathetic about applying for jobs, he would end up with a new Effect or philosophy at E: 'Being apathetic is self-defeating. I recognize that, in the past, I may have acted incompetently but I am not incompetent (gross overgeneralization). All human beings act incompetently on occasions. I acknowledge my assets — past and present experience, capacity for hard work, good relationships with colleagues and a steady work record. Accordingly, despite the redundancy, I am a person worthy of respect and esteem. I am determined to keep looking for another job; in the meantime I will lead as rewarding and productive a life as circumstances allow.' These types of adaptive cognitives, if firmly believed, will, according to RET theory, lead to behavioural and emotional changes. Although accepting the preferability of having employment and being concerned about not having it, with a new cognitive set the depression and anxiety should lift; the executive is now more likely to seek out opportunities and assert himself appropriately at interview.

One problem which could arise is the control of the ruminative patterns of anxiety-generating thinking. The individual may challenge the patterns as indicated above but may find, at least initially, that they return frequently. A valuable means of controlling such troublesome thoughts involves the use of a rubber band on the wrist. Immediately the troublesome thought occurs the individual extends the band 6–7 inches from the wrist and releases it to provide an aversive stimulus while, at the same time, emitting a subvocal 'Stop'; then the individual may challenge the thought or make some coping statement (see

Meichenbaum's work described later in the chapter); thus, the aversive stimulus is contingent upon the unproductive pattern of thought. This technique has the advantage of portability and can be administered discreetly in a variety of settings. It is lightweight, unobtrusive and self-administered; the technique can be used in close temporal contiguity with the anxiety-generating thinking. For the technique to be effective in controlling ruminative thinking it must be used consistently, that is on 100 per cent of occasions this type of thinking occurs. This method should not be overlooked because of its simplicity; many individuals report that this technique is extremely effective in the control of unwanted thoughts, ('worry'), and that, after a week or two, it is necessary to use the procedure only infrequently. Clearly, some care needs to be exercised in using the elastic band technique; should the wrist become red, move the band to the other wrist! Individuals frequently report that, after using the band for 2–4 weeks, it is rarely necessary to use it in the way outlined above; merely looking at it on the wrist is sufficient to disrupt the self-defeating patterns of thinking.

Another approach to dealing with problems of stress is stress inoculation. This is a coping-skills method developed by Donald Meichenbaum, Professor of Psychology, University of Waterloo, Ontario. This approach aims to develop the individual's competence to respond to stressful events in such a way that disturbing emotions are reduced and adaptive behaviour occurs.

Applied to the management of anger, the stress inoculation approach imparts anger control skills that, according to Professor R. Navaco, University of California, are of three basic forms: (a) preventative, (b) regulatory and (c) executional. The general objectives are to forestall anger from occurring when it is inappropriate, to help the individual regulate arousal and inappropriate cognitions when provocation results and to provide the individual with the skills required to cope with the provocation experience. The method does not aim to suppress anger, which can, on occasions, have positive functions. However, anger may become maladaptive when it occurs at undesirable frequency, duration and intensity; in some instances it may be more appropriate to be assertive than to express anger.

The term inoculation refers to a process of exposing the individual to manageable amounts of stressors; he is then taught the skills to manage the experience. There are two main stages in the process:—

(1) Cognitive preparation.

The role of cognitive preparation in the amelioration of stress reactions has been recognized for a long time; for example, it has been shown that this type of cognitive intervention used with surgical patients leads to improved adjustment during surgery, shorter duration to discharge and reduction in the use of drugs.

The anger control aspects of the cognitive preparation phase have certain similarities with the RET approach. Four aspects are recognized:

(a) instruction about anger arousal and its determinants;
(b) discriminating the situations which evoke the anger;
(c) identifying the adaptive and maladaptive aspects of anger;
(d) using the anger management techniques.

(2) Skill acquisition.
The individual first needs to learn how to modify his evaluations and expectations concerning provocations. It is of consequence that provocations are not given an exaggerated significance; the objective is to promote flexibility in the cognitive structuring of the circumstance that previously evoked anger. For example, a consistent evaluation of provocation as personal affronts is challenged; alternative assessments are considered. In addition, the individual concentrates on task orientation as opposed to 'personal insult' orientation, with a view to resolving the conflict.

Anger can be a consequence of inordinately high expectations of oneself and others. Thus, the goal is to lower the expectations to a more rational level and thereby modify the exaggerated importance ascribed to events. Meichenbaum's methods of self-instruction can be valuable in bringing about the desired changes in appraisal and expectations. Thus, self-verbalizations such as 'Don't personalize it' and 'He did not mean to act in this way' may be of value in the control of anger provided such verbalizations are congruent with the actual appraisal of the experience.

According to Novaco, the cognitive control of anger by means of self-instruction involves a sequence of stages:

(a) Preparing for the provocation.
This stage involves adjusting one's expectations to the demand and one's competency in response to the demand. Thus, it helps to establish a cognitive set that encourages evaluation of anticipated problems, not all of which can be fully predicted. However, some

individuals are prone to provocation and have chronic problems of anger control particularly with certain antagonists. By a process of careful monitoring, many situations likely to evoke anger can be predicted.

During the stage of preparing for the provocation, self-instruction for the regulation of anger could be of the following type: 'This could be a difficult situation but I can work out a plan to resolve it.'

'Concentrate on the issues; don't personalize it.'

(b)   Confrontation and impact.

This stage is concerned with the experience; the adoption of a problem-solving response mode is the goal. Self-statements at this stage might include:

'Just keep cool and remain in control of the situation.'

'It would be unproductive to lose control; think of what you have to do.'

'Find positive aspects to the situation; keep the cognitions reality-based.'

(c)   Managing the arousal.

This stage and the following stage allow for the possible inability of the individual at self-coping efforts. Rather than reacting automatically as in former styles of responding, the individual monitors his anger arousal; this serves as a cue to begin further coping efforts. Thus, self-instruction at this stage might include:

'My muscles are getting tense. Just tighten up all over, stretch the muscles and relax — let the tension go. Slow things down.'

'The anger arousal is the cue to take rational action. Time to introduce problem-solving methods.'

'Perhaps he wants to get me angry; let's keep my response reality-based; take it point by point.'

(d)   Subsequent evaluation.

Two possibilities exist:

(1)   The conflict remains unresolved; in this event the self-instructions are designed to mitigate self-arousal from ruminative patterns of thinking and may be of the type:

'Forget about the irritation. Ruminating about it will only result in further arousal.'

'Don't take the situation personally. Let's ignore it for the time being and don't let it interfere with the job.'

'Let's drop it for a period; then go back and look at the issues and possible solutions.'

(2) The conflict is resolved. Self-reinforcement is a component of this phase and is typified by statements such as:

'I am pleased about the way I handled the conflict.'

'I am approaching these conflicts rationally and I am getting better at it each time.'

'The confrontation was difficult but it was resolved without my getting angry.'

The goals of behavioural interventions in the control of anger are to provide skills which are incompatible with anger, to increase effective communication and to develop problem-solving skills.

Research indicates that reductions in physioloical arousal occur when the individual employs coping skills in confrontative situations. A moderated, task-oriented response in face of provocation is important. So too is the use of relaxation; relaxation counterconditioning is an effective means of treating anger. The objective is to inculcate a sense of self-control by mastering troublesome situations and internal states.

Self-monitoring of anger cues, whether internal or external, is an important aspect of control. The early identification of anger cues allows for the initiation of self-control efforts at the beginning of the chain of provocation when there is a higher probability of attaining control. Thus, the individual with anger control problems must use explicit cues to cope with the problem rather than reacting automatically to aversive experiences. Consistency of approach in using self-control techniques is crucial. Another point which needs to be borne in mind is that people with anger control problems tend to be quick to respond to aversive events. Impulse delay is essential; the delay provides the opportunity to marshal the coping strategies and to avoid aggressive over-reactions and escalation of the difficulty.

Effective communication is an important component in anger control; research indicates that persons with aggression problems lack adequate verbal skills. Competence in verbal communication is essential to the management of anger in confrontative situations. Assertive training can be of considerable value in that individuals with communication problems can be trained to express negative feedback in non-antagonistic ways which do not violate the rights of others.

Problem-solving strategies in the management of provocation are of considerable significance. Quite a few problems in the real world are ambiguous and lacking in essential facts and information. As a first step to resolving a problem the individual needs to:

(a) define all aspects of the situation operationally; defining the problem helps to identify the crucial stimuli that might increase the availability of an effective response; and

(b) formulate the elements appropriately; the individual in a problem-solving situation does not respond directly to external stimuli but rather to mediational cues; for example, the problem may be formulated as a conflict between a goal and some impediment standing in the way of that goal, or between two or more goals.

The second step in problem-solving is the generation of alternative solutions. The task here is to elicit a range of possible solutions among which may be found the effective ones. The Osborn (1963) method of brainstorming may be of value during this stage; the procedure is designed to generate ideas and has four ground rules:

(1) All criticism is ruled out. Thus, ideas are not evaluated at this stage.

(2) 'Free wheeling' is to be encouraged. Inappropriate ideas are welcomed.

(3) Quantity of ideas is required. The larger the number of ideas, the greater the likelihood of arriving at useful ideas.

(4) Cross-fertilization and development of ideas. Participants should indicate how the ideas of others can be improved or how two or more ideas can be developed into still another idea.

The third step in problem-solving is the decision-making phase; the previous stage will probably have generated a large number of options; if only one or two options have been generated the likelihood of selecting the most effective course of action is diminished. In evaluating the ideas attention needs to be paid to the likely consequences of each course of action and an examination made of the utility of these consequences in resolving the problem. In selecting the most appropriate strategy attention is focused on general courses of action likely to resolve the major issues but, in selecting the most appropriate tactic, the focus is on the likelihood of being able to competently implement the strategy. For example, in the situation where the executive has been made redundant, the evaluation of the strategy ('try to find an appropriate position') would depend on how well it would resolve his present predicament. The tactic ('contact a former school friend who is now a managing director of a large company') would be judged on the likelihood of him being granted an interview.

The final stage of the problem-solving sequence is the verification phase. Thus, the individual needs to evaluate the consequences of his actions and to match the outcome as he perceives it with the expected outcome. If the match appears to be satisfactory, the problem-solving process can be terminated. If, on the other hand, the match appears unsatisfactory, the cycle is repeated beginning with the definition of the problem.

By now it will be apparent that the major mode of action of the cognitive approaches is to modify the faulty patterns of thinking and the premises, attitudes and assumptions underlying these cognitions. Thus the individual, by identifying his thought content, idiosyncratic styles of thinking, emotional reactions and behaviour, can begin to understand their interaction. By consistently using the skills-oriented approaches advocated in this and other chapters the individual will be in a greatly improved position to manage his anxiety and anger responses and to become a more effective problem-solver when encountering day-to-day problems.

Chapter 7
Stress and Self-control

Many people expose themselves to stressors because of maladaptive habits. These may range from unsatisfactory work habits, such as a tendency to leave important tasks to the very last minute, or to behaviours which can have an adverse effect upon one's life expectancy, such as smoking. Excessive drinking, being overweight, engaging in frequent Type A behaviours, taking insufficient exercise, are all maladaptive habits which at best are likely to impair one's efficiency in the long run and at worst result in severe illness or premature death. Many of these behaviours, such as excessive drinking or smoking, are often themselves attempts to cope with a workload which is perceived as getting out of control. As coping strategies, of course, they offer only short-term benefits and the longer-term consequences are catastrophic.

Throughout history the problem of how one might overcome one's undesirable habits has been a popular preoccupation. Many solutions have been proffered, usually centring around the application of 'will-power'. Indeed, such notions have often offered paradoxical comfort to some people, the acceptance that they are totally lacking in will-power being taken to mean that there is therefore no necessity to struggle any further to overcome a habit when clearly they have no prospect of succeeding!

Fortunately, such concepts as 'will-power' and 'strength of character' have no place in the modern behavioural approach. There has been a considerable body of research evidence accumulated over the past 15 years concerning the problems involved in the changing of undesirable behaviours. The major factor to emerge has been the great importance which must be attached to the individual's ability to understand and discriminate events in his environment. The behavioural approach places great emphasis upon the relationship between a person's behaviour and his environment. In order to bring about change it is first necessary to know what events or cues precede the undesirable behaviours and what events, what consequences, follow from the behaviours. 'Behaviour' is defined very broadly in this context, to

84

include thoughts, feelings and images as well as overt, observable behaviours.

Goldiamond in 1965 emphasized the functional relationship between the environment and behaviour. In particular he emphasized the interdependence of behaviour and environment. That is, specific behaviours can be predictably controlled by the arrangement of specific environmental conditions. These can be imposed externally, or the individual himself can act in such a way as to modify his environment so that other relevant behaviours may be systematically changed. The behaviour to be changed is often referred to as the controlled behaviour, whereas the behaviours concerned with manipulating environmental variables are the controlling behaviours.

Traditionally, self-control has usually been taken to refer to situations involving restraint. Also the social desirability of the behaviour is usually a factor in whether or not it is taken to represent self-control. From a behavioural perspective the criteria for the definition of self-control are rather different than the usual ones. In the first place there will always be two or more behaviours which provide alternative modes of expression. The consequences of these behaviours are usually conflicting, and the pattern of consequences, that is whether they are pleasant or aversive in the short term or the long term, is usually different for the self-control behaviour compared to the undesirable behaviour. For example, if you wish to stop smoking, at any time you have the choice (a) to smoke, (b) not to smoke. The short-term consequences of smoking are pleasant, but unpleasant in the long term; the consequences of not smoking are the reverse. However, you may substitute an alternative behaviour, such as eating sweets; this behaviour will also have short-term and long-term consequences. In addition, there will be various environmental factors operating; for example if you are in a 'non-smoking' rail compartment it will be easier not to smoke, than if you are in a bar, et cetera.

By and large, self-control procedures are concerned with seeking either to increase or decrease some response. Usually, the behaviours to be increased have aversive short-term consequences but beneficial long-term ones, such as jogging, whereas behaviours to be decreased show the reverse pattern — short-term pleasant consequences with long-term aversive ones, such as smoking or over-eating. Some self-control measures have very long-term beneficial outcomes and therefore it is necessary to invoke the use of mediating symbolic factors to bridge the gap.

STAGES IN SELF-CONTROL

The first stage in setting up any self-control programme is the definition of what constitutes the problem to be tackled. The realization that smoking or obesity are in themselves major stressors and ultimately life-threatening, for example. The next stage is *self-monitoring*. This involves keeping records of the specific behaviour, the antecedent events and the consequences of the behaviour. For the first week or two the subject would merely be trying to collect *baseline* information concerning the problem behaviour. Then the treatment strategy is worked out and implemented. During this phase there will still be a need to engage in careful self-monitoring in order to establish that the procedures are being effective, and to take action if they are not.

There are several alternatives which may be implemented at this point; they comprise attempts to modify environmental factors, usually referred to as stimulus control, various self-reinforcing or self-punishing strategies and perhaps the use of internal or covert techniques.

Self-monitoring

Self-monitoring is the essential first step of any self-control programme, and remains at the heart of any attempt at behavioural intervention. Before any self-changes are initiated it is vital to obtain as accurate information as possible about the behaviour and the circumstances surrounding its occurrence, and the consequences following from the behaviour. Very often the individual finds the results of such an inquiry to be very surprising. For example, a person with a weight problem may confidently state that he eats very little food, taking very small meals, and he regards his tendency towards putting on weight as a great mystery, 'it must be due to my metabolism' being offered very frequently as an explanation. However, a properly carried out period of self-monitoring may reveal the very large intake of calories which takes place each day, the chocolate biscuits with the morning coffee, the sweets eaten on the train going home, et cetera.

Self-monitoring is also frequently reactive. That is, it constitutes a self-control technique in its own right. The very act of observing one's own behaviour changes that behaviour. Certainly some smokers find the act of obtaining their baseline smoking level sufficient to cut drastically their smoking consumption. When embarking upon a self-monitoring exercise the subject should be made aware that this is quite likely to change the behaviour concerned, otherwise he might be misled into some false attribution of the change. In order to make a self-observation it is necessary to make some sort of discrimination. The subject must be able to recognize the presence or absence of the particular response under consideration. This is easy when it refers to some easily measured response, such as smoking a cigarette or eating 50 grammes of food, but can be quite difficult when it relates to some covert event—the presence of a self-defeating thought, for example. People commencing a course of relaxation training will often complain, in the early stages, that the exercises are making them more rather than less tense. In fact they are not becoming more tense, but the exercises are designed to sharpen up their discrimination for tension, so an early effect is the recognition that one is tense, when previously one would not have been aware of this. Once having learned to recognize the presence of tension it is easier to do something about it. In Chapter 8, concerning biofeedback, the point is also made that a major aim of such training is to train the individual to discriminate internal cues, the training requiring external instrumentation initially, but the ultimate aim being the learning of physical cues. However, discrimination is merely the first step; it must be accompanied by an accurate form of recording procedure in order to provide the necessary information concerning antecedent circumstances and the consequences of the behaviour; it is also necessary for the target behaviour to be specified in detail so that its occurrence can be accurately pinpointed.

The precise timing of self-observation also needs to be specified. That is, should the recording be carried out at the time of the event or at the end of some predetermined period? For example, the recording of the urge to carry out some behaviour such as have a drink may in itself be sufficient to prevent the urge being acted upon. The collection of data of this kind provides an opportunity for self-evaluation on the part of the subject and also the setting of realistic goals. The latter point is one of very considerable importance. All too often people will set themselves goals of such difficulty that there is no realistic probability of reaching them. The subject then feels depressed and unworthy for having failed to reach these unrealistic goals and is quite likely to abandon the whole venture of self-change, whereas if a series of realistic goals had been set up from the outset then the subject would have experienced success in meeting these more modest goals and his self-control behaviours would have been strengthened.

Summarizing—self-observations recorded on a chart may often be useful as a reinforcing strategy, particularly if publicly displayed since this may contribute to change in environmental factors, for example praise from one's family for weight loss.

The means for recording will vary with the target problem. Often where a simple frequency count is all that is required some simple tally device will prove to be very useful, for example golf counters. It is usually necessary to draw up a record sheet which will simplify the collection of the necessary data. An example of a sheet to record smoking behaviour is given in Table 5.

Table 5 Smoking record

Day	Time	Amount	Comments
Monday	7–9 a.m.	5	1 in bed. Coughed 1 in station ⎱ 3 on train ⎰ Felt nauseated
	9–11 a.m.	6	Every 20 minutes during paperwork; felt tense.
	11–1 p.m.	4	2 during meeting; felt tense. 2 after lunch with coffee; felt relaxed.

In general the amount of information to be collected should be the minimum necessary for the given purposes and in as simple a format as possible. A simple wrist or pocket tally counter is to be preferred to paper and pencil if it will provide sufficient information. At the present time there is a lack of information concerning what precise effects various forms of self-monitoring may have, but future research will no doubt help to elucidate this point.

Although self-control programmes can be carried out by an individual entirely unaided it is often very useful if there is an external source of guidance. Many people are not very good at self-monitoring and therefore require training in both discrimination and recording of behaviour, and learning how to pinpoint in specific behavioural terms rather than in vague generalities. Such training can be enhanced by such techniques as modelling, reinforcement, and feedback of information concerning accuracy of reporting, et cetera.

How accurate the data may be will vary widely, not only with individuals but across situations, problems and recording systems. For example, insomnia is a common problem. However, obtaining accurate information about how much sleep people actually have is quite difficult. Accurate measurement can be made by having the individual attend a sleep laboratory, of course, where he can be wired up to recording equipment, but this might very well change his pattern of sleep. There is evidence to suggest that for people for whom sleep is not a problem there is a tendency towards overstatement of the amount of sleep they usually have, whereas insomniacs usually tend to understate the amount of sleep they have, which therefore accentuates the difference between the groups. Most behavioural studies of the treatment of insomnia utilize sleep latency—the time required to fall asleep—as the main measure, but this is open to many biases. In general, the simpler the measurement the better.

Self-monitoring represents the crucial first step in drawing up a self-control programme. As we have already said the act of self-monitoring will often bring about change in the problem behaviour. However, such change is often transient unless other strategies are adopted, such as self-reward, or some environmental change takes place which will serve to maintain the changes in behaviour.

Having carried out baseline measurement the next stage involves devising a suitable strategy or strategies for dealing with the problem behaviour. These may involve systematic changes in the environment, usually referred to as stimulus control or environmental planning. Another general approach is that of self-reward or self-punishment following some specific behaviour—there are also some specific covert methods. Self-reinforcement is usually referred to as behavioural programming. This includes the following:

(1) Positive self-reward.
    The bestowing upon oneself of a freely available reinforcer only after you have performed a specific behaviour. (For example, watching a favourite T.V. programme after completing one's jogging circuit.)
(2) Negative self-reward.
    The avoidance of, or escape from, a freely available aversive stimulus only after the performance of a specific behaviour.
(3) Positive self-punishment.
    The loss of a freely available reinforcer after the performance of a specific negative response. For example, sending a donation to a

least favoured political party after failing to reach a specific weight-loss target.

(4) Negative self-punishment.
Receiving an aversive stimulus after the presentation of a specific negative response. For example, receiving an electric shock from a cigarette case each time it is opened in order to take out a cigarette.

Stimulus control

Stimulus control procedures represent some of the earliest work in self-control. Basically, this approach is derived from laboratory studies which demonstrated that the probability of a response was influenced by the presence or absence of cues which had been previously associated with that response. Stimuli which are associated with the undesired behaviour are therefore reduced as much as possible. Stimuli associated with the desired competing behaviour are increased. Ferster and his co-workers first introduced these strategies in 1962 in relation to the control of obesity. They pointed out that many environmental cues become associated with eating behaviours. A person usually eats not only at the dining table, but in a variety of other situations. While reading, working, watching television, in the theatre, on a train, et cetera. Once the association has been established, then the individual may eat whenever he encounters these cues. Accordingly, eating was restricted to specific situations which occurred infrequently and no additional activities were allowed to accompany eating—for example reading. Emphasis was also placed upon competing incompatible behaviours to eating.

This technique has also been successfully applied to smoking, et cetera.

Self-reward

There has been considerable research into the effects of positive self-reward. In particular, one should note the work of Kanfer and Phillips (1970), and Bandura (1969). Their approach has focused on the three components of self-regulation: self-monitoring, self-evaluation and self-reinforcement. Bandura has worked within a social learning paradigm in which his subjects have observed some appropriate model engage in self-reinforcing behaviours and have then, at a later time, been placed in a situation in which they may engage in self-reinforcement.

Kanfer and his co-workers have conducted a considerable body of research investigating the development, maintenance and influence of experimental self-control patterns. For example, Kanfer has shown that stringent instructions for standards of self-reinforcement are necessary; lenient standards result in frequent and often inaccurate self-reward.

Self-punishment

As we have already pointed out there are at least two major types of self-punishment: (1) negative self-punishment; (2) positive self-punishment. The aim of either form of self-punishment is to reduce the occurrence of some particular behaviour. Additionally, one should distinguish self-punishment and other self-controlled patterns called restraint and endurance. A person displays restraint when he delays, refuses or reduces some form of positive stimulation, whereas endurance is shown when a person optionally tolerates some form of aversive stimulation. An example of endurance would be to continue with one's jogging routine in spite of being exhausted. The subject is aware of the ultimate positive consequences of his actions but, although he can anticipate them, they are clearly going to be delayed for some considerable period of time. The distinction between endurance and self-injurious behaviour, e.g. masochism, is quite a fine one. How such behaviour is perceived therefore depends very much upon the context. As to restraint, this is generally considered by the general population to be one of the major aspects of self-control. Indeed, the individual who can manifest such behaviour is often regarded as showing highly desirable character attributes.

The bulk of the research and application of self-punishment has been concerned with negative self-punishment. Much of the earlier work was concerned with the application of electric shock, but there was a wide variability in success. Elsewhere we have commented on the use of cognitive techniques and this approach has been utilized, for example, by Cautela (1967), in developing what is known as covert sensitization in which highly aversive imagery is paired with imagery of carrying out the undesired behaviour. This has been reportedly useful in controlling various behaviours such as smoking, or excessive intake of food.

It might be instructive to consider the application of self-control methods to various problem behaviours. This will illustrate how the strategies are applied.

SELF-CONTROL TREATMENT OF INSOMNIA

The behavioural treatment of insomnia usually encompasses two components: (a) some form of relaxation training, e.g. progressive relaxation or biofeedback assisted relaxation etc.; (2) stimulus control. A typical approach to stimulus control is that developed by Bootzin (1973). The stimulus control instructions are as follows:

(1)   Lie down intending to go to sleep only when you are sleepy.
(2)   Do not use your bed for anything except sleep; that is, do not read, watch television, eat or worry in bed. Sexual activity is the only exception to this rule. On such occasions the instructions are to be followed afterwards when you intend to go to sleep.
(3)   If you find yourself unable to sleep, get up and go into another room. Stay up as long as you wish and then return to the bedroom to sleep. Although we do not want you to watch the clock, we want you to get out of bed if you do not fall asleep immediately. Remember the goal is to associate your bed with falling asleep quickly. If you are in bed for more than 10 minutes without falling asleep and have not got up, you are not following this instruction.
(4)   If you still cannot fall asleep repeat step (3). Do this as often as is necessary throughout the night.
(5)   Set your alarm and get up at the same time each morning irrespective of how much sleep you have had during the night. This will help your body acquire a consistent sleep rhythm.
(6)   Do not nap during the day.

This approach has been shown to be effective with individuals who have had sleeping problems.

SELF-CONTROL AND OBESITY

There is very considerable interest in our culture in the problem of controlling weight. Since weight has been clearly shown to be a risk factor in the development of coronary heart disease, the control of weight should be given priority by busy executives who may well also have a whole range of other risk factors to consider.

Treatment approaches that have typically relied exclusively on following a particular diet have not been successful. Most people who do show rapid weight loss tend also to show rapid weight gain following the end of the dietary period. However, methods embodying the principles of operant self-control have shown some promise recently. Most successful reports had involved programmes which had been run by a therapist. Usually, they have consisted of 10 to 12 treatment sessions once a week, and more successes were reported from packages where the therapist is faded out during the treatment period. Baseline periods are often given relatively little attention since it is assumed that weight would not vary widely over a 1–2-week period and can be considered to have been relatively stable before the start of treatment. Most studies show a typical weight loss of about a pound per week and this seems to be a reasonably realistic level for most people to aim at. The initial stage then would be some sort of information package which would acquaint the subject with basic data concerning the effects of various forms of foods and which foods should be avoided.

Specific self-control techniques in relation to obesity would then include the following:

(a)   The removal of undesirable foods from the house, in particular the foods that require no preparation. This is following a package suggested by Stuart in 1978. The purpose of this is to make the time and effort involved in unplanned eating much greater.

(b)   The modification of eating behaviour. There is a good deal of emphasis upon changing one's actual eating habits. For example, putting one's knife and fork down on the table between each mouthful of food until the mouthful is swallowed, and possibly taking short breaks of up to 5 minutes during a meal in order to increase the client's perception that he does not have to eat the meal if a food is present on the table.

(c)   Stimulus narrowing. This is an attempt to narrow the range of available stimuli which can be associated with eating. The subjects are told that they must eat in only one room in the house and that they should not engage in any other activity while eating. That is, they should not watch television, listen to a radio, carry on a conversation or read while eating. There is evidence that many of these people are vulnerable to the effects of environmental cues. This was in particular pointed out by Schacter in 1971. He suggested that, in many of these people, eating behaviour is not triggered off by feelings of hunger but by the sight of food. Eating in a self-service establishment where there is a great abundance of different types of food is therefore likely to lead to over-indulgence.

Similarly, looking into the window of a well-stocked bakery which has a large variety of cream cakes on display may also trigger off the behaviour of purchasing and eating highly fattening foods. Stimulus control is therefore, of great importance with many obese subjects.

(d) Changing the stimulus environment. Subjects should try to expose themselves to stimuli that have tended to inhibit eating in the past; for example, eating in the presence of other people.

(e) Quality of self-reward. Clients should provide reinforcements for improvements in eating behaviour, such as eating smaller portions, eating appropriate foods, et cetera.

(f) Developing competing responses. The subjects should try to engage in competing behaviour whenever inappropriate eating might have been likely to occur. For example, going for a walk or drinking a large glass of water at a time when they would normally have started to nibble food in between meals.

(g) The use of shaping principles. The above principles should be incorporated into the programme gradually; Stuart recommended no more than one or two per week. The programme should be structured so that the subject has some rewarding experiences early in the programme rather than be faced with a series of very difficult tasks. Covert sensitization could also be included in the programme whereby the client might be trained to pair highly aversive imagery with images of eating some preferred but not desirable food, such as cream cakes.

Depending upon the individual's problems it may be necessary to incorporate other techniques into the programme such as cognitive techniques or assertive training etc. Programmes to control behavioural problems like obesity tend to require the use of an external counsellor or therapist in order to increase the probability of the subject sticking to the programme.

CONTROL OF PROBLEM DRINKING

One facet of self-control which we have not remarked upon so far is the interruption of chains of behaviour. Many behaviours are cued by stimuli associated with the behaviour immediately preceding it, and so on in a chain. For example, consider an executive who had a drinking problem, in that he always called at a bar on the way home in the evening and drank excessively. The behavioural chain would commence as he left his office, went to the car park, drove along a particular route which led past a particular bar, parking, going into the bar, ordering his drink, et cetera.

Although he might have the best intentions in the world of resisting on any particular occasion, by the time he has walked into the bar it would probably be extremely difficult indeed for him not to order a drink. At this point it is therefore too late in the behavioural chain to control this. Similarly, driving along the road towards the bar may, in itself, cue thoughts of having a drink and the general constellation of rewarding activities centred around drinking in the bar. It would be far more effective to disrupt the chain very early on—that is as soon as he leaves the office—by using another route home which does not involve passing any bars, or by using a different form of transport, or by giving a non-drinking companion a lift, for example. The important point to note is that the earlier in the chain, that is the more distant from the ultimate consummatory behaviour, the easier it is to perform a self-controlling response. This applies to any problem. There are many other features which would be part of a programme for problem drinking, such as an analysis of the actual drinking behaviour in order to see how it may be changed; or converting from spirits to some long drink, and learning to take small sips, rather than large gulps, in order to space out drinking more adequately. These changes can be conducive in producing a social pattern of drinking rather than a problem drinking pattern.

Success has been reported for the use of self-control techniques in problem drinking and obviously it is better to institute these procedures as early as possible in the development of the problem drinking. That is before the drinking has resulted in such devastating social changes as to make any amelioration of the problem much more difficult. By the time the drinking has progressed to the extent that there has been a split-up of the family, loss of job, et cetera, then the prospects that the client will be able to return to a full, creative, productive role in life are clearly greatly diminished. Once again this points up the need for an external counselling agency to be available to which employees can turn in confidence that this will not have any adverse effect upon their career. The young executive who has taken to excessive drinking in order to cope with pressures of work, and now realizes that he has a problem, should be aware of some avenue which would offer him a confidential and effective service.

OTHER AREAS OF APPLICATION

The concern with Type A behaviour, particularly in the United States, has recently led to programmes aimed at modifying these behaviours, again largely by the use of self-control and cognitive techniques. Subjects are being trained to re-evaluate their lifestyle and produce changes which can be expected to show long-term benefits. One obvious long-term benefit for both the individual and his company is avoidance of coronary heart disease! It is still too early to state how effective these programmes have been, but there is already the suggestion that there is considerable potential for development along these lines.

Self-control procedures can also be applied to developing and strengthening other useful skills such as improving one's work habits, or physical exercise habits et cetera. Indeed, again largely in the United States, considerable interest has been shown in the use of behavioural packages for the improvement of athletic performance. Sport Psychology has for some time been of importance behind the Iron Curtain, and is now achieving some prominence within the United States; the lessons to be drawn from this field are of considerable relevance to industry and commerce.

It is apparent that no single behavioural technique is likely to be a panacea. The use of these techniques needs to be carefully planned and evaluated and to form part of a rational approach. Where a problem is very straightforward then it is indeed possible for a person to work out and carry out his own programme, but by and large there is a clear need for a thorough behavioural analysis to be conducted by skilled personnel, a suitable programme devised, instituted and monitored. One can visualize the need for a Behavioural Unit both within and outside large organizations, to which employees could bring any sort of problem.

Chapter 8

Biofeedback and Stress

Biofeedback is the use of monitoring instruments to record and display information concerning physiological processes occurring in the body in order to allow the individual to gain voluntary control over the physiological processes. The concept of voluntary control of such processes as heart rate and metabolic rate is not new. For a long time travellers from the Far East have been bringing back intriguing stories of such feats, but it is only relatively recently that such possibilities have received serious scientific consideration. Until about 1960 it had been assumed that the autonomic nervous system, which is most intimately concerned in stress responses, could only be modified by classical conditioning. However, from the early 1960s onwards there was increasing interest in investigation of the possibility of modification of the autonomic nervous system by means of operant conditioning and these lines of research ultimately converged into the biofeedback movement. The term biofeedback itself came into use in 1969. The concept of feedback loops as controlling mechanisms had been well known in engineering and it was also known that within the body there were numerous closed feedback loops controlling physiological mechanisms. Biofeedback merely put the person as an observer and controller into this loop.

By the early 1970s biofeedback had attracted very considerable popular interest and many sensational and totally unfounded claims were being made in the popular press. However, throughout the last two decades, programmes of careful scientific work have continued, largely in the United States and, to a lesser extent, in the United Kingdom, to further our understanding both of the basic principles of the biofeedback process and to determine more precisely how these principles can be applied in clinical settings.

Essentially, there are three applications of biofeedback

(1) To learn to gain control over some physiological process which is not normally voluntarily controlled.

(2) To regain control over some physiological process over which control has been lost through injury or disease.

(3) To regain control over some physiological process over which control has been lost through injury or disease.

In the context of stress control it is largely categories 1 and 2 which will be considered. Category 3 is concerned with such applications of biofeedback as assisting patients to gain control over a limb which has been damaged in a road traffic accident resulting in loss of function. Another example would be helping patients gain control of limbs which have been paralysed following a stroke. However, although this is a rapidly developing and important area of clinical application of biofeedback principles, it is of less concern in the present context.

DEVELOPMENT OF BIOFEEDBACK

As has already been described, up to about 1960 there was a fixed belief that the autonomic nervous system could only be modified through classical conditioning and not through operant conditioning. It is rather curious why this belief came into being in the first place since there was never any systematic evidence to support it. However, the belief has now been discarded and there is no doubt that autonomic responses can be influenced by operant procedures. However, although such control has been established, the precise mechanisms underlying this are still far from clear. One such problem is that of mediation. This is concerned with the problem of whether the biofeedback responses are achieved by indirect mediation by some intervening system. That is, perhaps that effects are produced within the autonomic nervous system by means of some manipulation of the skeletal nervous system. We do have direct control over the skeletal nervous system; for example, we can move our arms or legs at will. Accordingly, for example, by holding one's breath or changing one's rate of breathing, it is possible to change one's heart rate. In an experiment endeavouring to investigate the operant control of heart rate it would, therefore, be possible for a person to apparently achieve some positive result by means of respiratory changes. Some investigators, notably Neil Miller (1968), have engaged in elaborate experiments in order to investigate this particular problem. Another form of mediation is by means of the manipulation of cognitive processes, that is by use of particular forms of imagery, thoughts and feelings. Once again, in the experiment which was seeking to produce, say, an increase in heart rate, it might be possible to do this by allowing the mind to dwell upon frightening images.

The investigation of potential mediational processes is one of the important lines of research being pursued at the present time.

By the 1960s the unsubstantiated belief that control of the autonomic nervous system by operant conditioning was impossible, was challenged. Various workers pursued different lines of research which, in the end, all converged by the late 1960s into the biofeedback movement. Each line of research tended to be followed by several groups of researchers working independently. For example, some workers were investigating the possibility of operant control of electro-dermal responses—that is, the changes produced in the electrical resistance of the skin or the electrical potentials recorded on the skin which were known to change in response to emotional stimuli. Indeed, the measurement and interpretation of changes in the electrical resistance of skin, commonly called GSR, the galvanic skin response, has long formed part of the so-called 'lie-detector', as used in the United States. When used as an indication of deception, the assumption has clearly been that changes in this particular physiological parameter are beyond the control of the individual and that the pattern of change will provide useful information concerning the emotional response to particular stimuli—for example, circumstances surrounding a crime. The possibility that these responses may well be capable of being brought under conscious control is clearly an interesting one in this context!

A second line was an investigation as to whether the human heart rate can come under operant control and again a number of workers independently investigated this possibility and were able to demonstrate that it was indeed the case that voluntary control could be obtained. In particular, Professor Brener (1966) was able to demonstrate operant changes in heart rate while controlling respiration by means of training his subjects to maintain their breathing at a constant rate using a metronome, while, at the same time, they produced changes in their heart rate in the required directions.

Other workers were investigating the control of electrical brain rhythms, particularly a slow form of brain rhythm called alpha wave. The alpha wave rhythm was thought to be related to a relaxed mental state and it is, perhaps, the work on the control of human brain rhythms which, more than anything else, caught the popular imagination and fuelled the more extravagant claims which were made for biofeedback in the early years of the 1970s.

Neil Miller and his colleagues were particularly concerned with trying to control the effects of mediation by the skeletal system and they conducted a very elegant series of experiments on rats which were paralysed by curare. By this means they hoped to operate directly upon the autonomic nervous system and they produced a very impressive series of experimental findings. For example, they were able to gain operant control of vasomotor responses in the ears of a rat, so that in one ear blood flow was increased and in the other ear blood flow was decreased. This resulted in a rat with one pink and one white ear! Unfortunately, there have been major problems in having these experiments reproduced in other laboratories, but nevertheless there is no doubt that the findings of Miller and his co-workers were one of the major spurs to further research by a great number of other people. By the early 1970s it was becoming very clear that biofeedback techniques could have a major role in combating various disease processes, particularly stress-related diseases. There has been a continuous research effort in this field ever since, which is continuing and constantly refining our knowledge concerning these processes.

TYPES OF FEEDBACK

There are various forms of feedback which can be used; for example feedback can be in various sensory modalities and convey varying amounts of information. There has been some attempt experimentally to define the most effective forms of feedback, but this is quite a complicated task and appears to depend partly upon the particular response being investigated, and partly upon such considerations as feasibility and convenience. Earlier work on the training of motor performance has suggested that knowledge of results is an important variable in the acquisition of motor skills and it has been amply demonstrated that such feedback should be rapid, consistent and precise. Indeed, continuous feedback is required when one is trying to control a rapidly changing variable.

In practice, feedback has tended to be largely in the visual or auditory modalities. For example, visual feedback could be a series of lights, a red light indicating change in one direction and a green light indicating change in another, or a graduated series of lights indicating both the direction and magnitude of change; or it could be a digital display where the numbers would give precise information about change, for example, a digital thermometer whereby the display would be the actual temperature and changes in either directions would be very easily seen. There is, therefore, a distinction to be made between binary feedback which merely indicates the direction, and proportional feedback which would give an indication of magnitude of change.

INSTRUMENTATION FOR BIOFEEDBACK

The qualities required in the instruments used for biofeedback depend very much upon the purpose for which they are being used. Quite clearly where research is being carried out into basic biofeedback mechanisms it is essential that the equipment is as accurate, reliable, and informative as possible. The operating characteristics of the equipment need to be precisely known in order that other investigators can produce the same results. Because of the very high quality of equipment required for research it follows this equipment is extremely expensive. However, once the basic research has been carried out and some particular application of biofeedback training has been established, then it is possible that less expensive equipment will be quite adequate for the clinical use in mind. However, the equipment must still be capable of accurately measuring the response involved and giving accurate and sensitive feedback back to the subject. An example of this is the work that is being carried out in investigation of the control of high blood pressure by biofeedback. Much of the American research has involved very complex, computer-controlled equipment which has cost many thousands of pounds. However, some extremely worthwhile work on clinical response of patients has been carried out by Dr Chandra Patel, a general practitioner in Croydon, using very simple equipment as part of her biofeedback and relaxation package. There is no doubt that very useful clinical results can be achieved by relatively inexpensive equipment.

USES OF BIOFEEDBACK

There are several different purposes for which biofeedback training might be appropriate. The first would be the use of biofeedback as a means of enhancing relaxation training in the learning of relaxation as a basic skill. The second might be biofeedback training of a particular parameter which seems to be of some importance in an individual's response to stressors. A third use would be as a therapeutic approach to some stress-related disorder.

The ability to relax should be regarded as a basic life skill. Undoubtedly, for an individual to devote a few minutes each day to the practice of some relaxation technique is a worthwhile investment. There are many techniques available for developing expertise in relaxation and many people are perfectly capable of achieving deep levels of relaxation without use of any biofeedback instrumentation. Nevertheless, there are people who do find it useful, particularly in the early stages, to have some objective feedback and measure of their progress. With all applications of biofeedback it is undesirable, at the end of the day, for a person to be dependent upon external instrumentation and there is always therefore an emphasis on training the individual to learn to focus attention on internal cues so that the external input of information from the instruments may be faded out. In this way individuals ultimately learn to monitor and regulate their internal states without the aid of external instrumentation and this, of course, helps in the process of a generalization of the learned responses. It is of great importance that individuals should learn to generalize their required skill into new situations and not merely learn to relax in one particular place. For general relaxation purposes of this sort, it is probable that electromyographic feedback is the most appropriate. That is feedback of the electrical activity arising from a muscle which is directly related to the level of tension in that muscle group. Electromyographic feedback is usually referred to as EMG feedback. However, other forms of feedback might be equally useful in this context. We shall return to this point later.

Whenever it is feasible it is preferable to obtain a profile of psychophysiological responses, both at rest and under a variety of stressors. The reason for this is that some individuals show what is known as a response stereotypy. That is, they show the same pattern of physiological responses no matter what the stressor. For example, some individuals may show the greatest response in the cardiovascular system by increasing heart rate and blood pressure and relatively small changes in muscle tension, whereas other individuals may show the reverse response. Such stereotypy is clearly apparent in patients suffering from stress-related disorders. That is, when exposed to a variety of stressors, patients who suffer from tension headaches, for example, will show greater changes in muscle tension than patients who suffer from high blood pressure. The latter will show greater changes in cardiovascular variables than the tension headache suffers. However, such response stereotypy is found in individuals who do not suffer from any clear-cut stress-related disorder.

It seems very plausible to assume that if individuals do show such a particular stereotyped response, and if their life exposes them to a significant number of stressors, so that this stereotyped response is frequently elicited, then in time they will develop a stress-related disorder involving the particular physiological parameter concerned in this stereotyped response. Where an assessment of psychophysiological profiles has revealed such a stereotyped response, then it seems most probable that biofeedback should be directed towards control of the physiological parameter concerned. For example, if a patient shows a stereotyped marked increase in blood pressure with each stressor, then the learning of a relaxation technique coupled with biofeedback aimed at the control of the cardiovascular system would seem to be the most appropriate strategy.

Biofeedback techniques have been developed to help in the treatment of many stress-related disorders, such as migraine, tension headaches, hypertension, gastric disorders, and so on. We shall shortly consider these in greater detail.

BIOFEEDBACK AND GENERAL RELAXATION

Interest in the teaching of general relaxation goes back several decades and some form of muscular relaxation has become an important component of behavioural approaches to many problems. Indeed, relaxation is often the key to the control of anxiety and tension in a great many situations which are difficult for people. Budzynski and Stoyva suggested, in 1969, that EMG biofeedback might be a suitable vehicle for producing generalized muscular relaxation. They suggested using the frontalis muscle in the forehead since it was thought to be a difficult muscle to relax and relaxation of this muscle would produce generalized physical and subjective correlates of relaxation. EMG biofeedback of this type has been widely used as a relaxation method although some authors have challenged the basic assumption that relaxation of the frontalis muscle induced by biofeedback does, in fact, produce generalized relaxation. Indeed, there has been some experimental evidence which does challenge the basic assumption. For example, there is a relatively low correlation between subjective feelings of relaxation and reduction in the objective level of tension in any muscle, and in particular in the frontalis. There is also a lack of correlation between changes in the level of tension in a trained muscle site and other more distant muscle groups. However, the evidence that orthodox relaxation training does produce generalized relaxation in all muscle groups is also somewhat thin. There has also been a challenge to the assertion that relaxation of muscle groups leads to a generalization of the relaxation process to other physiological systems, for example, the cardiovascular system. Recent work carried out by Arnarson and Sheffield (1980), however, has demonstrated that EMG biofeedback to the frontalis muscle can result in changes in emotional states, and also generalization across a number of physiological parameters in subjects with relatively high levels of tension.

From these studies it would appear that EMG biofeedback is a more efficient means of producing this form of relaxation response than is feedback of hand temperature. The current evidence favours the view that relaxation can be taught by training in some straightforward relaxation exercises following a modified Jacobsonian approach coupled with EMG biofeedback.

BIOFEEDBACK AND STRESS-RELATED DISORDERS

There are a number of common disorders which appear to be stress-related. These include high blood pressure, migraine, tension headaches, gastric disorders, et cetera. There are also these and other disorders which appear to be exacerbated when individuals suffering from them are exposed to a variety of stressors and which then serve as further stressors themselves, thus further increasing the stress response. An example of this would be the knowledge that one's efficiency was being impaired by experiencing a severe tension headache and this would lead to further impairment of one's performance. Obviously, migraine and tension headaches fall into this category; another example would be dysmenorrhoea which also appears to have severely adverse effects upon work and academic performance in women.

There is little doubt that disorders of this type are multifactorially determined. Sufferers should certainly consult their physicians and it is also preferable that a behavioural analysis should be carried out in order to try to determine what other factors may be implicated in the maintenance of a disorder. For example, allergic responses to common foods may be of some importance in the onset of a migraine attack. Alternatively, a headache may be maintained by the presence of the headache helping the individual avoid some unpleasant social duty.

Disorders of this kind may be very obtrusive in a person's life — such as migraine headaches — or the sufferer may be blithely unaware of the presence of a disorder which nevertheless may pose a major threat to the individual—for example high blood pressure. Many people are completely oblivious of high blood pressure and the condition often comes to light in the course of some routine medical investigation, either an annual health check carried out in an occupational health setting or perhaps as a result of a check for insurance purposes. The situation sometimes arises that although the condition is free of obvious symptoms, treatment of the condition often does give rise to unpleasant side-effects. In these circumstances the individual may well not be highly motivated towards continuing with treatment and thus increasing the risk of further undesirable consequences. Biofeedback research has suggested various directions in which these disorders can be combated, and we shall now consider these approaches in more detail.

BIOFEEDBACK AND HEADACHES

Headaches are a very common experience, several surveys showing that the majority of people suffer a headache at least once a year. The economic and personal costs of headache can, however, be substantial. Reduced work performance, time off work, et cetera, are all the results of severe headaches.

Headaches have traditionally been divided into tension headaches, where it is assumed that the major component was due to excessive tension in the muscles of the head and neck, and vascular headaches such as migraine, where the assumption was that there was some underlying disorder of blood flow in the head. There has always been a recognition that many people suffer from some mixed form of headache. At the present time there is some controversy concerning whether there are qualitatively different forms of headaches or whether headaches are better regarded as lying on a continuum. Headaches diagnosed as migraine tend to have particular associated symptoms. They are frequently preceded by prodromal symptoms, such as visual disturbances, jagged lines across the field of vision; the headaches themselves are often accompanied by nausea and perhaps vomiting and sensitivity to light so that the victim withdraws into a darkened room. The headaches may be prevented by the use of vasoconstricting drugs. However, these symptoms also tend to be associated with severe headaches and Claire Philips (1978) has argued, on the basis of surveys carried out in general practices in London, for the continuum hypothesis with headaches differing in intensity resulting in headaches being labelled as tension headaches at one end of the continuum and migraine headaches at the other.

There have been a number of studies indicating a correlation between headache onset and increase in muscle tension, particularly in EMG activity recorded from the frontalis muscle; for example, a study conducted by Sainsbury and Gibson in 1954. A number of other early studies also produced the same results but more recent studies, again particularly by Philips, have failed to demonstrate this effect.

Budzynski and his co-workers in the early 1970s found a significant increase in the resting level of muscle activity in people who had frequent and severe tension headaches, and this study finally has been replicated by a number of people. Budzynski and his co-workers (1973) suggested initially that EMG biofeedback appeared to be an effective treatment for tension headaches. However, biofeedback as a treatment method appears to be no more effective than relaxation, although it is not known whether different individuals might respond better to one or other treatment approach. Budzynski *et al.* (1973) reported on a large number of patients who had received biofeedback treatment for tension headaches and claimed that 80 per cent of the individuals treated had substantially reduced their headaches. There have not been many long-term follow-up studies conducted so far but the evidence to date does suggest that the treatment effects of tension headaches are long-lasting. Certainly, a study reporting on a follow-up at 1 year showed that the improvement had been maintained.

The evidence to date does suggest that people who suffer from frequent and severe tension headaches could benefit from appropriate psychological treatment and could probably learn to dispense with much of the pain-killing medication they might have been accustomed to taking. In practice, it is usual for the subject not only to receive EMG biofeedback training but also to be encouraged to practise some relaxation technique at home using a relaxation tape.

Biofeedback training sessions

The subject will first of all learn to reduce his frontalis EMG to a low level, initially by using feedback; later he will be trained to maintain a low level without the use of feedback by means of a fading procedure whereby the feedback is gradually phased out. It is obviously essential that individuals should learn to relax their muscle tension using internal bodily cues and not have to rely for this information upon external instrumentation. The final purpose of any biofeedback training programme is to generalize the results of the training outside the clinical situation into the real world, and the subject will be trained in a variety of techniques to help with this generalization.

Migraine headaches

There is little doubt that migraine headaches have plagued humanity for a very long period of time. Estimates of the prevalence of migraine headaches in the population varies somewhat but some studies have suggested that up to 10 per cent of the population have experienced this form of headache. It has already been noted that there is a certain amount of controversy surrounding the problem of whether headaches are really qualitatively different but various symptom patterns have been defined to describe various types of migraine. Classical migraine is one in which there is a clear-cut prodromal period in which the subject experiences sensory or motor symptoms such as flashing lights, jagged lines, other disturbances of the visual field, tingling or numbness in the limbs. The headache is unilateral and is accompanied by nausea and possibly vomiting; there is sensitivity to light. Common migraine is the term given to a similar headache without the prodromal symptoms. Cluster headaches are brief headaches which tend to appear in clusters, hence the name. There are also headaches in which the neurological symptoms persist after the headache itself has passed. In general, migraine headaches are more severe than tension headaches. The mechanisms underlying this sort of headache are still not entirely clear. However, it is thought that the prodromal signs follow a sequence which begins with vasoconstriction of the blood vessels in the head. This reduces the blood supply to the nerve cells in the brain so that these function abnormally and the severe head pain which follows is thought to begin with a period of vasodilation which appears as a rebound. Though there is a good deal of evidence broadly supporting this view of the general chain of events, there has been some conflicting data and the situation is clearly rather more complex than this rather simple view would suggest. One early suggestion was that people who suffer from migraine tend to have a fairly permanent state of peripheral vaso-constriction between headaches, so they were described as having cold hands and feet and, although there are many clinical anecdotal reports to uphold this, there is now some evidence to suggest that this is not universally the case. Similarly, the role of specific precipitants of migraine attacks has also proved a somewhat thorny issue. With some people there do appear to be undoubted relationships with diet, and other people show a clear-cut relationship with exposure to stressors. In other people the onset of migraine appears to be associated with escape from environmental stressors; patients showing 'weekend migraine', are commonly encountered in any clinic. Though some people appear to be able to function as long as the stressors are present, upon their removal they are frustrated by their headaches. At the very time when they should be relaxing and recuperating, such as at weekends or during holidays, they are unfortunately likely to suffer from these extremely severe headaches.

In addition to the presumed vascular response underlying these headaches, there is some evidence, again notably from Philips, that patients suffering from migraine headaches may also have high levels of muscle tension. Indeed, there is a suggestion that in some migraine sufferers their muscle-tension level may actually be higher than that of some patients suffering from tension headaches. The biofeedback treatment of migraine has been used as an attack upon the presumed vascular mechanisms associated with the condition. Treatment has mostly focused upon skin temperature feedback, seeking to increase the temperature of the fingers. Visual feedback of skin temperature of the fingers has normally been used and patients have been trained to increase this temperature thereby decreasing vasoconstriction in the periphery of the body and increasing blood flow through the hands. This treatment is usually also coupled with home-based practice of some other relaxation technique. Most studies have also incorporated the use of autogenic training as part of the relaxation package. Many patients who suffer from migraine do complain of having cold hands and feet, particularly in winter, and temperature training, accordingly, will be seen to be a much more plausible treatment for people showing this particular pattern of symptoms. The object of the training would be to get them voluntarily to increase their skin temperature to over 30°C. Many migraine sufferers find this particularly difficult and it may well take many sessions before they achieve success at hand-warming. Certainly the evidence does suggest that treatment for the migraine type of headache tends to be more prolonged and intensive than that for tension headaches. Subjects trying this form of treatment therefore require a good deal of support and encouragement, particularly throughout the early stages; the use of a variety of behavioural approaches is to be recommended. Where there is evidence of high levels of EMG activity it is also helpful for these subjects to be trained in the production of low levels of EMG from the frontalis muscle by means of EMG feedback.

There is ample evidence that patients who, in particular, suffer from severe and long-standing migraine attacks, can be greatly helped by means of biofeedback and relaxation training packages. A reasonable quality temperature training equipment is rather cheaper than EMG biofeedback equipment and is tending to be becoming increasingly available. Obviously, the treatment of all forms of headaches remains a domain for further research but given the present state of knowledge there is no doubt that people can, in general, be greatly helped to cope with these disorders and in many cases to avoid them altogether, by means of biofeedback and associated techniques. The investment of time in learning what in any event should be regarded as an essential skill in living, is clearly amply justified. Not only can individuals greatly increase work productivity and general creativity, but they can also avoid a good deal of personal misery, and inconvenience and discomfort, inflicted on their families and their work associates.

BIOFEEDBACK AND HYPERTENSION

High blood pressure is a major problem in the Western World. Estimates of the prevalence of high blood pressure in the population vary quite widely but figures as high as 20 per cent of the adult population in the United States have been thrown up by some studies. There are many causes of high blood pressure, such as damage to the kidneys, et cetera, but the bulk of hypertensives suffer from a form of the illness called essential hypertension where there is no obvious organic pathology producing the disorder. A wide variety of factors are known to influence blood pressure, such as age, sex, body weight, dietary habits, et cetera. There is also clear evidence that any increase in blood pressure leads to a decrease in life expectancy. Major causes of death in people who suffer from untreated high blood pressure are heart failure and stroke. There is good evidence that if high blood pressure is reduced through suitable treatment, then there is an increase in life expectancy.

There is no clear definition of what constitutes hypertension, since there is a continuum of blood pressure readings and the point at which treatment is initiated is an arbitrary one and will vary from physician to physician. However, as has been pointed out, there is very good evidence that any increase in blood pressure increases a risk of serious disorders. Many people show a fluctuating, mild increase in blood pressure and this condition is often referred to as labile or borderline hypertension. There is evidence that suffering from this condition also enhances one's medical risks.

Some patients show marked cardiovascular changes as part of their stress response, and in particular an increase in blood pressure. If they are frequently faced by stressors in their day-to-day life, then this response is frequently elicited and for long periods of time their blood pressure may be elevated. It is thought that this ultimately leads to the internal mechanisms which regulate blood pressure resetting at a higher level so that the blood pressure no longer returns to its previous habitual low level but now returns to a higher resting level. This process may be frequently recycled, leading to higher and higher levels of blood pressure which sooner or later lead to further physical complications. Medical treatment of the condition is clearly indicated in high levels of hypertension and there is a certain amount of controversy between doctors as to which would be the most appropriate point at which to commence treatment. Treatment is pharmacological, there being a variety of potent drugs with different modes of action which have all proved successful in controlling high blood pressure. The earlier drugs tended to be frequently associated with undesirable side-effects but this has been less of a problem recently although some people do show an idiosyncratic response to drugs. Where, as is often the case, the raised level of blood pressure did not produce any unpleasant symptoms for the patient, whereas the medication did, there is a strong tendency not to continue with the medication. It is also well known that there are major compliance problems in expecting people to take medication on a regular basis and, indeed, many busy people living harassed lives often simply forget to take their medication. Where one's physician feels that medication is necessary, the individual should comply with the medical requirements, but any additional technique which can help reduce the amount of drugs being ingested, can give additional protection, or can help an individual manage altogether without drugs is clearly desirable This then is the role for biofeedback and associated techniques.

Blood pressure is usually recorded as systolic pressure over diastolic systolic representing the maximum pressure as the heart forces the blood out into the arteries, and diastolic being the low point between beats. There is currently no general agreement concerning the relative seriousness of rises in either the systolic of diastolic pressure; in general individuals tend to show rises in both and there is good evidence that a rise in either is undesirable. Some studies have used a cuff device with a microphone to measure systolic and diastolic levels and to give feedback directly of blood pressure to the patient. Some of these studies produced relatively small-scale changes but many did produce significant drops in both systolic and diastolic pressures. In general, however, using this technique, training has had to be extended over a large number of sessions. Studies throughout the early 1970s generally demonstrated that biofeedback training was more effective than just using relaxation training, although the latter tended to produce a drop in blood pressure. In general the drawback with direct feedback of blood pressure is that the equipment is cumbersome and expensive, and in order to obtain a good result it has usually been necessary to have rather intensive training.

Patel and North (1975), in an interesting series of studies, were able to demonstrate that a package consisting of a yoga type of relaxation training, coupled with an indirect biofeedback of electrodermal activity, produced a significant drop in blood pressure in patients suffering from hypertension. Patel was also able to demonstrate that this could lead to a reduction in medication for these patients. Sheffield (1981) has also used in indirect form of biofeedback, that is, skin temperature measured from the fingers, with a group of hypertensive patients. Again, the biofeedback was part of a package including relaxation training. Sheffield demonstrated that, using this package in an occupation health setting, it was possible for most subjects to reduce blood pressure to their normal limits. This study consisted of 20 minutes of training conducted at weekly intervals in an occupational health centre located within an industrial complex. The subjects were a mixed group of executives and workers who had been identified as suffering from hypertension by means of an annual health check, and who were then offered this treatment in conjunction with whatever treatment their general practitioner felt advisable. The vast majority of subjects were able to produce significant reductions in their blood pressure using this package; both systolic and diastolic showed significant falls. This study is of interest since it demonstrated that this form of treatment could be offered from within the resources of an occupational medical centre and produced very little disturbance in the working routine of the participants. By contrast, attendance at a special hospital clinic would have entailed at least half a day's loss of work. The package used by Chandra Patel and her associates could also be very easily transposed to an occupational health setting. Chandra Patel in fact carried out most of her studies within a general practice setting.

Biofeedback had also been compared to various other techniques in addition to straightforward relaxation training. There have been studies looking at the effects of autogenic training, usually also coupled with muscle relaxation. Hypnosis has also been used, and there is evidence that any of these techniques can be effective; finding which technique would be most suitable for which particular subject is an empirical question.

It is clear that hypertension is a condition with very serious consequences for the individual and for the organization within which the individual works. In addition to pharmacological intervention, it is quite clear that people can be helped by various psychological methods, including biofeedback. Biofeedback does have the advantage of being relatively easy to fit into the work environment of, say, an occupational health centre and therefore the possibility now exists of providing techniques to individuals working within an industrial complex which has demonstrated its efficacy and which would cause minimal disruption to individuals' working routines. One would imagine that there is now a clear case for large organizations to be implementing behavioural stress prevention programmes.

OTHER AREAS OF APPLICATION

There have been large numbers of other conditions to which biofeedback techniques have been applied. For example, the treatment of gastric disorders; asthmatic attacks; Raynaud's disease, in which the patient suffers painful coldness in the extremities, et cetera. These are all thought to have a strong relationship to stressors, and biofeedback can normally be used as part of a stress-coping programme. There is also a rapidly developing major clinical field of application of biofeedback in the treatment of neuromuscular disorders. Although these techniques are more likely to be applicable to a hospital population, again they could well find an area of application in an occupation health setting. Certainly in the case of a senior executive troubled by some neuro-muscular disorder, it would clearly be highly beneficial for appropriate techniques to be readily available. A further condition which has afflicted many executives who have come to the clinical attention of the authors is 'writers' cramp'. This is a term which covers quite a large number of different problems, all of which are characterized by excessive tension in one or other of a group of muscles involved in writing, either in the hand or, more commonly, the forearm, although the excessive tension can often extend into the shoulder. Biofeedback of EMG from the appropriate muscle sites has often proved to be quite dramatic. Additionally, the use of biofeedback, particularly EMG feedback, may be very useful in leisure activities. Either as a general relaxation technique or where excessive tension of particular muscles is proving disadvantageous; for example, to a golf swing or a tennis service, et cetera. Improved performance at such leisure activities might be an important factor in improving the general morale of busy executives labouring under a variety of stressors, and may greatly enhance their everyday work performance.

ADVANTAGES OF BIOFEEDBACK

A concept that has arisen in recent years is that of 'locus of control'. This is concerned with whether an individual sees himself captain of his own destiny or merely some helpless plaything of fate. That is, whether he has an internal locus of control and feels that he can influence his life and what happens to himself, or whether he has an external locus of control and cannot influence events and has to suffer whatever 'slings and arrows of outrageous fortune' come his way. The tendency in the Western World has been towards an external locus when it comes to medical matters. People, as it were, see that there is some defect in their body and take it along to the doctor to be repaired. Indeed, they often give the impression they would like to leave their body and call in and collect it in a couple of days' time by appointment when everything has been put right. The modern medical emphasis on wonder drugs and magic bullets has tended to reinforce this attitude and led to a certain passivity in the population. The behavioural approach, to the contrary, particularly as exemplified by biofeedback, very much encourages the individual to play a major part in his own treatment. He is given guidelines on how to conduct himself but the onus is very much upon him carrying out required activities and accepting responsibility for himself. Biofeedback is very clearly concerned with the *control* of physiological functioning. Of all the behavioural techniques, perhaps biofeedback reveals this particular characteristic in its clearest form. This makes biofeedback often the most appropriate choice of strategy with certain problems. A hard-headed executive, goal-oriented, and used to dealing in quantitative data, may reject out of hand suggestions that he might undertake some strategy such as relaxation training. If he did undertake it, the concrete benefits would very rapidly make themselves known but such individuals may be prone to reject these possible approaches without sampling them first. They may see the whole proposition as being far too nebulous. Biofeedback, by contrast, with its emphasis on instrumentation and the display of precise, accurate information, could have the advantage of appealing to individuals of this particular temperament and once they have grasped the essentials of this technique it is much easier for them to grasp behavioural principles in general and see how other strategies could enhance creative functioning. For this reason, even where there is no clear-cut evidence for the superiority of biofeedback over what are superficially cheaper techniques, such as straightforward relaxation training, there is still a case to be made for the provision of biofeedback equipment. To be attached to a suitable biofeedback machine is to be left in no doubt whatsoever of the clear association between mental events and physiological events, and the potentiality that is offered by the concept of control over these processes. Senior management in particular are likely to be of the type who require evidence for any proposition, but once having been given it are very likely to act upon it. All senior managers should have the opportunity of being challenged by biofeedback and other behavioural approaches.

As we have seen, biofeedback has a variety of roles to fill and deserves an important place in any stress prevention programme.

Chapter 9

Vulnerability, Coping Skills and Personal Stresses

Brief reference has been made in previous chapters to the four elements that are ultimately bound up together in stress reactions. One of these might be called the basic disposition or temperament of the individual, and the second is the extent to which that person possesses the skills to deal with life's vicissitudes. The third factor, clearly, is that of the actual stresses and strains that are, have been, or will be imposed on that individual; while the fourth is what has been called the Type A personality.

Clearly these four elements combine together to produce some resultant, and one must know about all of them in order to predict a particular outcome. Prediction is one thing, control is quite another, and it is evident that one can do something about factors 2 and 3, whereas factor 1 is less amenable to influence, and there may be limitations to what can be done about factor 4. Certainly, where the behavioural approach is concerned, the emphasis should be upon the acquisition of coping skills and the possible rearrangement of environmental conditions as a means of offsetting the effects of stress. We have tried to present cogent discussion of these two possibilities in this book.

Since these four elements are involved, however, it is reasonable to gain some idea of one's personal standing on each and, in the following pages, a guide to such assessment is provided. You should not regard this as a test but simply as a rough and ready signpost to what your relative personal standing may be on those factors.

First, let us deal with the basic temperamental variable, sometimes referred to as emotional stability. All of us have a position to occupy on this dimension; those of us at the higher level have a greater sensitivity to noxious events, while at the lower end, of course, the sensitivity is reduced. Pavlov, the Russian physiologist, noted such individual differences in his experimental animals and used the terms 'strong' and 'weak' nervous systems to denote the two ends of the continuum. On the scale, which is reproduced in Table 6, checking a majority of items in the positively keyed direction might suggest the existence of a tendency to be on the vulnerable side of average, while checking only one or two may indicate low vulnerability. For the former, stress reactions could be more readily produced to a given set of psychological pressures; such people might be better advised to acquire strong coping strategies and to examine their commitments with a view to reducing environmental demands (see Chapter 1).

Table 6   Basic vulnerability/stability

1. A tendency to suffer from frequent headaches.
2. The feeling of being constantly under a strain; never feeling very relaxed.
3. Being excessively tired much of the time, never feeling sufficiently rested and refreshed by sleep.
4. Sensations of pressure in the head, feeling tight bands around the head.
5. A feeling of lacking energy, drive; having to summon up reserves of energy to do quite ordinary things.
6. Tremor, perspiration excessive, heart beat races.
7. Poor sleep, nightmares, restless sleeper.
8. Feeling generally strung up and tense without any real reason for this.
9. Finding that things 'get on top of one' too easily; making heavy weather of everything.
10. Finding that one's feelings are too easily hurt; excessively sensitive when compared to others.
11. Always seeming to find something to worry about.
12. Sitting down to relax and finding oneself dwelling on negative aspects of the past and the future.
13. Being very aware of bodily processes, heart thumping, pains, pins and needles, et cetera.
14. Over-reacting to life's small problems; making mountains out of molehills at home and at work.
15. Expecting the worst to happen when the 'risk' is very small; e.g. never feeling happy until all the family are 'safely' at home.
16. Wanting to ring the office when on holiday to make sure everything is all right.
17. Taking everything that goes wrong 'personally'.
18. 'Jumpiness' when telephones rings or some minor extraneous noise is heard.
19. Unable to concentrate well at home or at work; being distracted by unwanted and irrelevant thoughts a good deal.
20. Experiencing surges of fear, anxiety or panic sensations for no apparent reason.
21. Feeling very indecisive, taking a long time to make decisions, putting things off that have to be done.
22. Feeling that many things in one's life are simply getting out of control — one is a helpless victim of circumstances.

Table 7   Actual stress checklist

---

1. Actually having so much work to do that it must be brought home most nights and weekends.
2. Actually having inadequate subordinates whom one has to chaperone, protect, or put up with.
3. Actually having a poor product or poor service to offer, that worries you.
4. Actually having to work with others of unpredictable and uncertain temperament.
5. Never having time for a real break during the day, even for a few minutes.
6. Actually having to assume responsibility for events over which you have no control at all.
7. Actually working under very tight time pressures.
8. Actually having a wife/husband who does not get along very well with colleagues and their partners.
9. Having superiors make excessive demands.
10. Actually spending too much time away from home.
11. Not enjoying one's job.
12. Physical health is poor.
13. Having no-one on whom one can depend at work or at home.
14. Having very real financial problems.
15. Having a number of continuing domestic problems that remain unresolved.
16. Having sexual needs that are largely unsatisfied.
17. Having no time for developing personal hobbies and interests.
18. Having no real chance to express oneself or make own contribution at work.
19. Not getting along well with wife.
20. Having problems with one's children.
21. Unsatisfactory prospects at work; blocked promotion, poor career development, possible redundancy, et cetera.
22. Not having appropriate level of knowledge or expertise for the job one is doing or expected to do.
23. Having a job that makes little or no use of one's abilities and skills.
24. Unable to take a real holiday last year.

The second list (Table 7) includes items that constitute actual problems in the life of the individual. It is argued that these operate in a kind of additive manner to increase the stress load on the individual. The items obviously include matters that may be highly interactive with those involved on other scales, hence the term 'actual' is used to remind one that this represents the true state of affairs rather than that it simply *feels* that it is an accurate description of one's predicament. For example, working under time pressures (item 7) may be a feeling induced by one's sensitivity (vulnerability) or be self-induced (Type A behaviour) rather than something intrinsic to the job operation itself.

Coping strategies are, in a sense, self-explanatory, involving the kind of self-corrective behaviours that reduce the stressful impact of life's vicissitudes (see Table 8). Life events provide all of us with ample opportunity to hyper-react; some of us appear already to possess strategies that help us to deal with these inevitable and unavoidable bumps and bruises and the checklist included here focuses upon some of these 'skills'.

Examples of Type A behaviour (see Chapter 1) are said to define the group of individuals likely to suffer from stress-linked diseases, such as coronary heart disease. The evidence for the existence of a Type A personality is still, however, somewhat tentative and it may well turn out to be an amalgam of the variables set out in the three scales already mentioned. To an extent, it may be that what is called a Type A person has a native disposition to act impulsively, neurotically, or belligerently (see Table 9); to some extent such behaviour may be a demand characteristic of many modern working environments. A best guess is that these behaviours probably represent a critical interaction between a constitutional disposition and environmental prompts and reflects, as one medical consultant said in describing to us his client's problem, '. . . the tendency to live at 100 miles an hour'.

Of course these are only examples of the types of items that would constitute the scales in question; they represent checklists that serve to provide the sense of what is involved. It will be apparent that there is overlap between the items that comprise the scales and, as has already been said, anyone scoring highly on the scale of basic vulnerability will be very likely to have higher scores on actual stresses (they will be sensitive to such matters and tend to perceive them as applying) and lower scores on coping skills.

These items may serve as a useful reminder about the kind of problems one may experience and, perhaps, act as an incentive to deal with some of them. They may also, however, serve to draw attention to the way in which the personal qualities and characteristics of the individual do or do not allow an effective adjustment to be made. Although exposed to stressful circumstances, sound temperament and a good level of coping skills will enable some individuals to deal with a most exacting environment; while for others, even small stress loads will prove to be too much.

In our view, however, it is important to focus upon the aspects of the stress situation about which something can be done; the actual stresses

Table 8 Coping skills

---

1. I can work quickly when needed, but take my time when there is no need to rush.
2. I never feel a sense of guilt when taking time off.
3. I can control my temper; when I lose it, this is calculated and I don't go beyond what I intended to say or do.
4. I can leave my work and relax.
5. I am able to look at a pile of work to be done and not get 'thrown' by it, or get a panicky feeling that I'll never manage.
6. If something does not happen just when I expected or wanted it to I can simply get on with something else and 'forget' about the unfinished thing.
7. I can focus on one thing at once and clear my mind of other things to be done.
8. I can usually get other people to see all sides of a problem.
9. I can take a measured look at a job to be done without feeling an urge to rush into action before getting things properly thought out.
10. I can unwind quickly on holiday and begin to enjoy myself from the start.
11. I can get over disappointments without getting too upset; I recognize that one cannot have everything the way one wishes.
12. I can forget my mistakes without too much difficulty, recognizing that not everything goes the way one wants it to.
13. I can let go and enjoy my relaxation time.
14. I am able to turn my mind from one problem to focus on another without the former getting in the way.
15. I do not let worries get out of hand; my worries are constructive/problem-solving rather than negative restatements of the problem.
16. I can usually strike some kind of acceptable balance between what I want and what others expect.
17. Giving negative feedback to subordinates is not too difficult.
18. I can usually deal effectively with aggressive people so that the heat is taken out of the situation.
19. I am able to give my view without being over-assertive in most situations.
20. I am able to tell other people what I feel and think; I do not simmer privately or explode.
21. I can delegate; I do not take something on myself rather than ask a subordinate to take on an extra chore.
22. I can say 'no' when a colleague makes an unreasonable demand, without getting into conflict.

Table 9　Type A characteristics

I get involved in a great many different ideas and projects.
I am very ambitious.
I drive myself harder than do others.
I work long hours from choice.
I get impatient and angry with incompetence and inefficiency.
I enjoy competing at work and elsewhere.
Deadlines are very important to me.
I have my finger in many pies.
I have plenty of battles on my hands at work.
I do not suffer fools gladly.
I take pride in getting the job done faster than most.
Having to tolerate delays is very irritating to me.
I prefer to assume complete responsibility, rather than share it with others.

---

to which individuals are exposed and the level of coping skills possessed. We have indicated in this book that there are a number of fairly simple strategies that can make a considerable difference to the amount of stress actually experienced, the emphasis being upon a behavioural approach to acquiring physiological, cognitive and motor habit control.

What we have said so far in this book, however, has been directed towards increasing personal understanding of behavioural strategies and their application; there remains something to be said about the way in which organizations themselves might direct attention to the causes and cures of stress reactions among employees. Our experiences of acting in a consultative capacity to various organizations suggests that there are a number of possibilities to be considered.

STRESS-PROBLEM IDENTIFICATION

In small office settings it is often quite easy to become aware when close colleagues are experiencing some adverse change in state, and it is not usually difficult to detect when that state has become sufficiently protracted and intense to require attention. We would not argue, of course, that every minor alteration in mood or circumstance should lead at once to the application of remedial assistance; such attempts are, in any event, often misguided. Furthermore, we would be in favour of allowing individuals to have some opportunity to exercise their own coping abilities when problems come along so as not to encourage the development of dependent reactions.

Nevertheless, it is not too difficult to secure a consensus of opinion when the time for intervention (perhaps initially of a more informal type) has arrived and some kind of help has to be offered. But, as we have noted, while quite a refined judgement can be made in the small-office situation, awareness that a problem has reached critical proportions may be less obvious in the larger work unit.

One of the ways in which this problem may be overcome is that of increasing the awareness of, and sensitivity to, stress reactions by including appropriate courses as part of other aspects of training programmes. We are not suggesting that the workforce as a whole should be exposed to such courses and, indeed, there is no need for this. We would, however, strongly advocate increasing understanding and awareness of stress problems at appropriate management levels; a greater sensitivity to such problems as they arise serves, in our view, to secure more effective action and less disruptive and damaging consequences.

Mr J., a 55-year-old company director, experienced a prolonged psychological reaction following a period of considerable work stress. The work of the company for which he had personal responsibility had increased very greatly and a variety of technical problems had occurred; he felt that his fellow-directors had failed to offer the support to which he was entitled and had allowed him to carry by far the greatest workload. This was objectively true and his colleagues were certainly solicitous and concerned when Mr J.'s 'breakdown' occurred. Problems had arisen in part from Mr J.'s own unwillingness to concede that he was not able to cope, but his colleagues were culpable in failing to recognize obvious signs that something was wrong. The result was that Mr J. required a considerable period of time away from his work and found it difficult to attain his old level of effective functioning even after resuming work again. In our experience this kind of situation occurs frequently, and certainly more often than need be the case.

The awareness and sensitivity that is required to identify problems of this kind do not call for any special intuitive powers but, in our view, can be conferred by quite brief exposure to appropriate teaching.

Such training would obviously include information on the causes of stress, personal coping methods, the control of stress by organizations, 'people management' problems, and so on, although we would not envisage that such training would equip individuals in the organization to deal with all such problems in a professional way. Rather, the aim would be to increase awareness and understanding in the area of stress prevention and management, so that recognition of these problems can be made sufficiently early and appropriate referral action can be taken as necessary.

REFERRALS FOR SPECIALIST ATTENTION

Having drawn the above conclusion, however, we would not argue that the large organization has no part to play in offering practical help in stress prevention and stress management. Indeed, many companies do offer this kind of help and it can, on occasions, be highly sophisticated and effective. Indeed, we would strongly advocate setting up appropriate machinery, perhaps within the medical or personnel departments of large organizations to which individuals could have ready access. We would see this arrangement as helpful in a substantial number of cases where constructive advice and, perhaps, a limited counselling service may be sufficient.

However, we have been most impressed by the reservations entertained by company personnel in respect of stress problems. In our experience this is not so much true of the more 'public' difficulties, e.g. there is no hesitation in confessing one's distaste for identifying an individual for redundancy, or having a 'showdown' with a colleague. But such problems, while admittedly not particularly easy to deal with, appear to carry an almost binding social obligation to feel bad about tackling them and there is little reluctance to discussing this possible source of stress in a public way. The same is true, of course, in respect of overwork since, within limits, there is a certain kudos to be gained from the concession that one is working sixteen hours each day.

While we do not wish to give exaggerated emphasis to the point, it is our firm impression that the more seriously debilitating stresses tend to be private in character and are not likely to be ventilated within the company. There is, rather, a desire to avoid such matters becoming known to the company, even when the organization has provided facilities for confidential exchanges on such matters.

There are, of course, obvious reasons for this reluctance; that the information will be 'leaked', and that this will affect the individual's future within the company, or that the necessary expertise does not exist locally, or that a genuinely independent 'hearing' will be denied, and so on.

We feel very strongly that the stress-affected individual should have access to sources of help outside the company, that he or she can recognize as both expert and independent. We have noted, for example, that the company-sponsored workshop on the problems of stress can be guaranteed to produce a crop of private requests for help even where the company concerned has developed useful facilities for this type of help.

In our view it is essential that companies should establish machinery by which personnel might approach some outside consultancy. Obviously, setting up this machinery would have attendant problems. If the company is assuming financial responsibility for the facility then some check upon its operations would be needed and, hence, an aspect of privacy could be affected. Furthermore, it is not difficult to appreciate that even an independent organization may, on occasions, feel that there are wider obligations than those to the stressed individual and may wish to have some agreed means of dealing with a problem having serious consequences for the company concerned. These and other difficulties require discussion and, perhaps, different solutions in particular cases; but they do not affect the general conclusion that the resolution of many stress problems requires the use of an independent, confidential consultancy with acknowledged expertise in the field of stress, in addition to the facilities provided by the company itself.

SELECTION PROCEDURES

We have argued, in this chapter and elsewhere in this book, that the acquisition of coping skills and the careful appraisal of one's commitments can be of critical importance in avoiding stress. We have, however, pointed to the importance of constitutional vulnerability in determining the degree of sensitivity or robustness that the individual may bring to the work situation and, in our view, the selection of key personnel should take this factor into account.

Selection procedures understandably take many things into consideration and, rightly, give emphasis to existing skills, knowledge and past achievement. Most accord a high degree of importance to personal qualities, although it is not often that any attempt is made to assess them in any objective way, and we strongly advocate the use of recent developments in the objective assessment of vulnerability where key company posts are involved. There is ample evidence from one's personal experience and other sources, including media reports, to alert one to the problems that may be created by placing the potentially unstable individual in positions of great responsibility and there is little need to offer further justification here.

It could be argued, of course, that the introduction of a deliberate attempt to assess emotional stability and vulnerability, and to use such assessment as one of the criteria for selection, is to be resisted. Such arguments, for example, may take the form of stating that it is wrong to assess attributes that the individual has no capacity to control, that the assessment is irrelevant to abilities and knowledge, that the methods employed are not foolproof, or that this inquiry concerns a private area of functioning and should not be part of a public selection procedure. We would take the view that such assessment is essential since the outcome of erroneous selection may have profound implications for the individual himself, for the company, and perhaps for the employees of that organization. We would go further and argue that such selection is included anyway, but is usually tacit, more subjective and less likely to operate fairly. In short, we would argue that there is an excellent case for employing modern psychological technology in the screening of applicants for highly responsible positions, and that companies have a responsibility to ensure that this is done.

MONITORING FUNCTIONS

By and large it is our experience that organizations react to stress problems when these have reached a critical level by virtue of their generality or intensity. We have already argued that it is far better to deal with such problems by the creation of appropriate agencies both within and external to the organization concerned. Even when this has been done there is still a need for the company involved to have a finger on the pulse, so to speak, by becoming better informed about the way in which its structure, its operations, and its workforce generate particular or general types of stresses.

This should be the task of some individual (or perhaps unit in the case of very large organizations) who would have the responsibility of evaluating the stress potentials involved within that organization. While idiosyncratic examples of stress are of interest and, of course, would be dealt with ideally in the way described above, getting a broader picture of where and how stresses are generated in an organization demands the continuous monitoring of such matters and involves the compilation of data over lengthy periods of time. Clearly, problems arise out of such an operation since organizations can change in many ways and make interpretation of data more difficult and, additionally, record-keeping of this kind can carry an undesirable degree of information dissemination. It is a matter for discussion how these monitoring functions are performed and perhaps the operation would need to be somewhat different in the varying contexts involved.

REDUNDANCY COUNSELLING

Problems arising from redundancy are particularly common at the moment and it is obvious that little has been done to take account of them. Indeed, for the most part it has not been thought possible to do more than arrange a satisfactory financial cushion for the individuals involved.

This kind of limited conception of a problem is certainly not peculiar to industrial and commercial organizations. A few years ago an investigation of patients in hospital 'terminal' wards revealed that many individuals were suffering from severe depression; it is not, of course, that this discovery came as any great surprise but the view was generally current that a severely depressed state is 'understandable' since these people have only a short time to live. What simply had not occurred to many of those involved in their treatment was that something might actually be done to relieve the oppressive mental state.

Similarly, a rather more positive attitude towards redundancy, other than simply throwing money at those affected, is called for. Quite often, it seems, the state of mind induced among the redundant ranges between panic and acute depression, and real support and help is required. Organizations should assume, we feel, a degree of responsibility for setting up a counselling service to provide this kind of assistance, perhaps linked to whatever financial provisions and job prospect evaluations are made available.

There is, of course, much to be done by way of relieving stresses and, understandably, the financial cost will be substantial. However, in our view such investment would enjoy a high return in terms of securing many obvious benefits of a tangible, as well as a more intangible, kind.

References

Arnarson, E. O., and Sheffield, B. F. (1980). *Generalisation of Biofeedback Training*. Proceedings of the Annual Conference of the Biofeedback Society. Colorado Springs.

Bandura, A. (1969). *Principles of Behavior Modification*. New York: Holt, Rinehart & Winston.

Benson, H. (1975). *The Relaxation Response*. New York: Morrow.

Bernstein, D. A., and Borkovec, T. D. (1973). *Progressive Relaxation Training*. Chicago: Research Press.

Bootzin, R. R. (1973). A stimulus control treatment of insomnia. Paper presented at the American Psychological Association Convention, Montreal.

Brener, J. (1966). Heart rate as an avoidance response. *Psychological Record*, **16**, 329–36.

Budzynski, T. H., and Stoyva, J. M. (1969). An instrument for producing deep muscle relaxation by means of analog information feedback. *Journal of Applied Behaviour Analysis*, **2**, 231.

Budzynski, T. H., Stoyva, J. M., Adler, C. S., and Mullaney, D. J. (1973). E.M.G. biofeedback and tension headache: a controlled outcome study. *Psychosomatic Medicine*, **35**, 484–96.

Burns, L. E. (1981). Relaxation in the management of stress. In: *Coping with Stress* (Editors: Marshall, J. and Cooper, C. L.). London: Gower.

Cautela, J. R. (1967). Covert sensitization. *Psychological Reports*, **20**, 459–68.

Ellis, A. (1955). *How to Live with a Neurotic*. New York: Crown.

Ferster, C . B., Nurnberger, J. L., and Levitt, E. B. (1962). The control of eating. *Journal of Mathematics*, **1**, 87–109.

Friedman, M., and Rosenman, R. (1974). *Type A Behaviour and Your Heart*. New York: Knopf.

Goldiamond, I. (1965). Self control procedures in personal behaviour problems. *Psychological Reports*, **17**, 851–68.

Jacobson, E. (1938). *Progressive Relaxation*. Chicago: University of Chicago Press.

Kanfer, F. H., and Saslow, G. (1969). *Behavioural Diagnosis in Behaviour Therapy: Appraisal and Status* (Editor: Franks, C. M.). New York: McGraw-Hill, pp. 417–444.

Kanfer, F. H. and Phillips, J. S. (1970). *Learning Foundations of Behaviour Therapy*. New York: Wiley.

Lang, P. J., and Lazovick, A. D. (1963). A fear survey schedule for use in behaviour therapy. *Behaviour Research and Therapy*, **2**, 27–30.

Lindsley, O. R. (1964). Direct measurement and prosthesis of retarded behaviour. *Journal of Education*, **147**, 62–81.

McFadden, C. (1977). *A Year in the Life of Marin County*. New York: Alfred A. Knopf.

Meichenbaum, D. (1977). *Cognitive-Behaviour Modification*. New York: Plenum.

Miller, N. E. (1968). Visceral learning and other additional facts potentially applicable to psychotherapy. *International Psychiatric Clinics*, 294–312.

Novaco, R. (1975). *Anger Control: The Development and Evaluation of an Experimental Treatment*. Lexington, Mass: Heath.

Osborn, A. F. (1963). *Applied Imagination*. New York: Scribners.

Patel, C. H., and North, W. R. S. (1975). Randomized controlled trial of yoga and biofeedback in the management of hypertension. *Lancet*, 2:93–5.

Paul, G. L. (1966). *Insight vs Desensitization in Psychotherapy: An Experiment in Anxiety Reduction*. Stanford: Stanford University Press.

Philips, C. (1978). Tension headache. *Theoretical Problems*, **16** (4), 249–62.

Rahe, R. H. and Arthur, R. J. (1978). Life changes and illness studies, past history and future directions. *Journal of Human Stress*, **4**(1), 3–15.

Sainsbury, P., and Gibson, J. G. (1954). Symptoms of anxiety and tension and accompanying physiological changes in the muscular system. *Journal of Neurology, Neurosurgery and Psychiatry*, **17**, 216–24.

Schacter, S. (1971). Some extraordinary facts about obese humans and rats. *American Psychologist*, **26**, 129–44.

Sheffield, B. F. (1981). Thermal Biofeedback in the Control of Hypertension. (Unpublished).

Stuart, R. B. (1978). *Act Thin. Stay Thin*. London: Granada Publishing.

Wolpe, J., and Lang, P. J. (1964). A fear survey schedule for use in behaviour therapy. *Behaviour Research and Therapy*, **2**, 27–30.

Additional Reading

Argyris, C. (1971). *Management and Organisational Development: The Path from XA to YB*. New York: McGraw-Hill.

Beech, H. R. (1969). *Changing Man's Behaviour* (Pelican Original). Harmondsworth: Penguin.

Beech, H. R. (1978). Learning: cause and cure. Chapter 6 in *Stress at Work* (Editor: Cooper, C. L.). Chichester: Wiley.

Birk, L. (Editor) (1973). *Biofeedback: Behavioural Medicine*. New York: Grune & Stratton.

Brown, B. B. (1977). *Stress and the Art of Biofeedback*. New York: Harper & Row.

Bruno, F. J. (1980). *Behaviour and Life*. Chichester: Wiley.

Chapman, A. J., and Jones, D. M. (Editors) (1980). *Models of Man*. Leicester: British Psychological Society.

Chesney, M. A., and Roseman, R. (1980). Type A behaviour in the work setting. Chapter 7 in *Current Conceptions in Occupational Stress* (Editors: Cooper, C. L. and Payne, R.). Chichester: Wiley.

Ciminero, A. R., Calhoun, K. S., and Adams, H. E. (1977). *Handbook of Behavioural Assessment*. New York: Wiley.

Coelho, G. V., Hamburg, D. A., and Adams, J. E. (1974). *Coping and Adaption*. New York: Basic Books Inc.

Cooper, C. L., and Marshall, J. (1980). *White Collar and Professional Stress*. Chichester: Wiley.

Dearnaley, E. J., and Warr, P. B. (1979). *Aircrew Stress in Wartime Operations*. London: Academic Press.

Duncan, K. D., Gruneberg, M. M., and Wallis, D. (Editors). (1980). *Changes in Working Life*. Chichester: Wiley.

Eysenck, H. J., and Wilson, G. D. (1976). *A Textbook of Human Psychology*. Lancaster: MTP Press.

Gatchel, R. J., and Price, K. P. (Editors). (1979). *Clinical Applications of Biofeedback: Appraisal and Status*. New York: Pergamon Press.

Goldfried, M. R., and Merbaum, M. (Editors). (1973). *Behaviour Change Through Self-Control*. New York: Holt, Rinehart & Winston.

Hamilton, V ., and Warburton, D. W. (1980). *Human Stress and Cognition*. Chichester: Wiley.

Hersen, M., and Bellack, A. S. (1976). *Behavioural Assessment*. Oxford: Pergamon Press.

Hilgard, E. R., Atkinson, R. L., and Atkinson, R. C. (1979). *Introduction to Psychology*, 7th edition. London: Harcourt, Brace Jovanovich.

Lawler, E. E., Nadler, D. A., and Carmann, C. (1980). *Organisational Assessment: Perspectives on the Measurement of Organisational Behaviour and the Quality of Work Life*. Chichester: Wiley.

Lazarus, R. S. (1966). *Psychological Stress and the Coping Process*. New York: McGraw-Hill.

Likert, R. (1967). *The Human Organisation: Its Management and Value*. New York: McGraw-Hill.

Mash, E. J., and Terdal, L. G. (1976). *Behaviour Therapy Assessment*. New York: Springer.

Sarason, J. C., and Spielberger, C. D. (1980). *Stress and Anxiety*, vol. 6. Chichester: Wiley.

Selye, H. (1976). *The Stress of Life*. New York: McGraw-Hill.

Thoreson, C. E., and Mahoney, M. J. (1974). *Behavioural Self-Control*. New York: Holt, Rinehart & Winston.

Ursin, H., Baade, E., and Levine, S. (1978). *Psychology of Stress*. London: Academic Press.

Williams, R. L., and Long, J. D. (1975). *Towards a Self-Managed Lifestyle*. Boston: Houghton Mifflin.

Woodworth, R. S., and Sheehan, M. R. (1967). *Contemporary Schools of Psychology*. London: Methuen.

Yates, A. J. (1980). *Biofeedback and the Modification of Behaviour*. New York: Plenum.

Author Index

Subject Index

131